Music of Christendom

The Music of Christendom: A History

Susan Treacy

IGNATIUS PRESS
San Francisco

AUGUSTINE INSTITUTE
Greenwood Village, CO

Cover art: Lorenzo Pasinelli, *St. Cecilia*, Oil on canvas, Private Collection
Cover design by Ben Dybas

© 2021 by Ignatius Press, San Francisco,
and the Augustine Institute, Greenwood Village, CO
All rights reserved.
Hardback ISBN: 978-1-950939-24-4
Paperback ISBN: 978-1-950939-21-3
Library of Congress Control Number 2021937708
e-Book ISBN: 978-1-64229-175-9
Printed in Canada ∞

Contents

Prelude

Is music something that merely expresses emotion, as many people believe? Is it something ephemeral, something mystical, beyond description? Is it something frivolous, something purely for entertainment? Or does music embody and represent a rational order? As we traverse the history of Western music, we will examine how some of the above questions were answered at various points in history.

In *The Idea of a University*, Saint John Henry Newman wrote:

> Music, I suppose ... has an object of its own.... It is the expression of ideas greater and more profound than any in the visible world, ideas, which centre indeed in Him whom Catholicism manifests, who is the seat of all beauty, order, and perfection whatever, still ideas after all which are not those on which Revelation directly and principally fixes our gaze.[1]

Newman was not writing about sacred music, per se, but about music in general. As a violinist, he had direct experience with music; add to that his superb intellectual powers and his personal holiness, and it is clear that the above quotation has an immense authority. Joseph Pearce's words echo Newman, and they remind us that

> the age of Christendom corresponds to the finest flowering of civilization. It is an age in which becoming civilized (holy) is the

---

1   Saint John Henry Newman, *The Idea of a University* (New York: Doubleday, 1959), 111–12.

only means of attaining the perfect civilization of Heaven. It is, therefore, hardly surprising that the heart of Christendom— its theology, its philosophy, its painting, its architecture, its sculpture, its music, its literature—is the very incarnation of the integrated harmony, wholeness and oneness, of its Founder.[2]

In one sense, this book will be the story of Christendom, but told through its music. We shall travel the musical landscape of Christendom, stopping at various points and pausing to study selected masterpieces of music in their cultural contexts.

It is convenient—but not always accurate—to assign names and dates to different musical style periods. The Renaissance era in music history did not end at 11:59 P.M. of the year 1599; nor did the Baroque era begin at midnight of 1600. There is considerable overlap in musical styles, as well as in the philosophies that accompany them. Also, the chronology of style periods in music does not always equate with style periods in literature and the visual arts.

This book will cover not only vocal music, whose words have the ability to form us in virtue, but also instrumental music, whose varied tones have, in themselves, the capacity to affect us. The works discussed in this book are favorites of mine, and many of them are works that will amplify your understanding of the faith.

At the end of this volume is a list of one hundred masterworks that every Catholic should know. Indeed, there are so many marvelous composers, genres, and masterworks of classical music that it has been a challenge to decide which ones to feature.

---

2   Joseph Pearce, *Literature: What Every Catholic Should Know* (San Francisco: Ignatius Press; Greenwood Village, CO: Augustine Institute, 2019), 3.

It is hoped that this book will be an encouragement to learn more about the great tradition of Western classical music, the music of Christendom, and above all, that it will encourage the reader to listen!

Let's close this prelude with a quotation by Joseph Ratzinger (the future Pope Emeritus Benedict XVI). The Holy Father, who is a classical music lover and pianist, has written about art and music many times, and here he is playing another variation on the same theme, the theme of Christ as the source of beauty, that beauty that civilizes and sanctifies.

Next to the saints, the art which the Church has produced is the only real "apologia" for her history. It is this glory which witnesses to the Lord, not theology's clever explanations for all the terrible things which, lamentably, fill the pages of her history. The Church is to transform, improve, "humanize" the world—but how can she do that if at the same time she turns her back on beauty, which is so closely allied to love? For together, beauty and love form the true consolation in this world, bringing it as near as possible to the world of the resurrection. The Church must maintain high standards; she must be a place where beauty can be at home; she must lead the struggle for that "spiritualization" without which the world becomes the "first circle of hell."[3]

---

3   Joseph Cardinal Ratzinger, *The Feast of Faith: Approaches to a Theology of the Liturgy*, trans. Graham Harrison (San Francisco: Ignatius Press, 1986), 124–25.

Musical Wisdom of the Ancient Greeks and the Transmission of the Classical Legacy to Christendom

As Ovid recounts in his *Metamorphoses*, Orpheus was such a virtuoso singer and player of the lyre that none could resist the power of his music. When an asp bit his bride, Eurydice, on their wedding day, Orpheus descended, lyre in hand, to Hades to retrieve her. Ovid's version of the tale does not mention the various personalities who would try to keep Orpheus from reaching the infernal deities, but it does include Orpheus' impassioned plea, sung before the god of the underworld (unnamed by Ovid) and his wife, Persephone. These monarchs and their shadowy court were moved and granted Orpheus' request to release Eurydice on the condition, however, that he not look back at her. We know, alas, that he did look back at his wife and that she receded into Hades. This familiar legend is iconic for its depiction of the power of music through the Greek concept of *ethos*, the idea that music can influence the emotions and morals/behavior of the listener.

Little actual music—only about forty fragments—survives from ancient Greece. Thus, how can Greek civilization have had such an important influence on Western musical culture? The answer is that far more writings *about* Greek music survive, plus depictions of Greek music-making in visual art (sculptures and vase paintings). For the Greeks, the term "music" (*mousike*) meant more than just melody (*melos*)—or sounding music. It also encompassed poetry, since most music—which was monophonic, consisting of a single, unison melody line—was vocal. Any instrumental accompaniment usually merely doubled the vocal line but could be embellished. Influential writings have come down to us from philosophers, such as Plato and Aristotle, and music theorists, such as Pythagoras, Aristoxenus, and Cleonides.

Tertullian's familiar question, "What does Athens have to do with Jerusalem?" might well be asked when the question of music arises. The earliest Christians were Jews, but after Saint Paul began preaching to the Gentiles, the Church took a new direction. The first Gentile, Greek-speaking Christians were mostly from the poorer classes, and they responded readily to the Gospel of Christ, which offered them hope. As time went on, however, evangelists approached Gentiles of the more prosperous, educated classes who, steeped in philosophy, demanded a more intellectual approach and sought for reasons to believe.

Was there anything of pagan Greek philosophy that could be synthesized with Christian truth? A number of writers applied themselves to this question, and Christianity became enriched by a selective incorporation of ancient philosophy. As for music, there were two interrelated philosophies that were appropriated from Greek philosophy by Christian writers. Disciples of Pythagoras who lived in the sixth century B.C. spread his idea that numbers were a key to interpretation of the cosmos. In the second century, for example, the neo-Pythagorean Nichomachus gave an account of how Pythagoras discovered musical numerical ratios while walking by a blacksmith's shop. He was intrigued by the sounds of hammers of different weights striking the smith's anvil. After noting the various weights of the hammers, Pythagoras went home and made his own experiment using weights. As a result of this he invented the monochord, a simple instrument of one string stretched across a box. He could then divide the string by stopping it with a finger, thus creating harmonic ratios. The resulting divisions of the string yielded the following ratios, which correlate to intervals: 2:1 = an octave; 3:2 = a fifth; and 4:3 = a fourth. The story is a mixture of fact and fiction because the ratios in the story can only apply to the length of strings, not to the weight of hammers. Nevertheless, these ratios were correct and formed the basis for the future development of music. Thus, Pythagoras and his disciples are said to have discovered the numerical correlations determining the fundamental intervals of music—the octave, the fifth, the fourth, the second.

Rhythms, too, were regulated by number because each longer note could be reduced to a basic duration. Thus, with musical intervals and rhythms being so closely allied with numbers, they instantiate the Greek idea of *harmonia*. This term, connoting well-ordered unity of different parts, had more than one meaning and could refer to philosophical concepts, mathematical proportions, societal structures, a musical interval (the distance between two pitches), scale type, or melody type. From here it was possible to extend the concept of musical ratios to the planets. The distances of the planets from each other, as well as their movements, were thought to be compatible with certain notes, musical intervals, and scales. As a result, the idea arose of the harmony of the spheres—that the planets, as they revolve, produce sounds that the human ear cannot perceive. For now, we won't say much more about Pythagoras, but we shall see that his influence was transmitted to Western culture, and we will see it manifested at various points in our narrative.

One later example of Pythagoras' enduring influence can be seen in Shakespeare's *The Merchant of Venice*, when Lorenzo speaks of the harmony of the spheres to Jessica.

There's not the smallest orb which thou behold'st
But in his motion like an angel sings,
Still quiring to the young-eyed cherubins;
Such harmony is in immortal souls;
But whilst this muddy vesture of decay
Doth grossly close it in, we cannot hear it.[1]

This Pythagorean idea of the musical and numerical under-girding of the universe had further ramifications, for if *harmonia* of the cosmos was governed by music, then it stood to reason that music could also affect the *harmonia* (harmony) of the human soul. *Musica humana*, according to the Pythagoreans, was this harmony between the body and the soul. Plato, in *Timaeus* (47e), describes this concept.

Harmony, which has motions akin to the revolutions of our souls, is not regarded by the intelligent votary of the Muses as given by them with a view to irrational pleasure, which is deemed to be the purpose of it in our day, but as meant to correct any discord which may have arisen in the courses of the soul, and to be our ally in bringing her into harmony and agreement with herself; and rhythm too was given by them for the same reason, on account of the irregular and graceless ways which prevail among mankind generally, and to help us against them.[2]

Music, thus, has the ability to instill harmony into the soul—a testimony to music's ability to affect human conduct. Plato, in his treatises *Republic* and *Laws*, discusses this ethical power of music in terms of the educative value of the *harmoniai* (in the sense of modes, or scales) and the importance of keeping

---

1   William Shakespeare, *The Merchant of Venice*, ed. Joseph Pearce, Ignatius Critical Editions (San Francisco: Ignatius Press, 2009), 5.1.60–65. (Numerals refer to act, scene, and line.)
2   Translated by Benjamin Jowett (Project Gutenberg, 2008), https://www.gutenberg.org /files/1572/1572-h/1572-h.htm.

pure the various genres of music and poetry. According to Plato, the Dorian and Phrygian *harmoniai* were the most valuable in the education of the governing classes because the *ethos* of these modes cultivates the virtues of temperance and fortitude. Plato extols music's educational value but cautions that the boys' education must contain an equal mix of music and gymnastics, and he cautions against innovations in music.

In the *Laws* (770a–701c), Plato discusses various genres of music and the immemorial practice of not mixing them. He complains that now, in his own time, uneducated and disrespectful men have "contaminated laments with hymns and paeans with dithyrambs, actually imitated the strains of the flute on the harp and created a universal confusion of forms."[3] Now audiences have appointed themselves judges of what is best, based solely on what they like, thus initiating a trajectory of lawlessness that ends in anarchy and misery. Clearly, Plato sees that music has the ability to affect human behavior either for good or ill. Aristotle, in his *Politics*, laid out his own theory of imitation, whereby music that imitated a particular *ethos* would produce that same *ethos* in a listener. Many composers, especially in the seventeenth and eighteenth centuries, would have Aristotle's theory in mind, in order to move the emotions of their listeners.

These philosophical concepts from the Greeks would prove to be influential in the forging of Christendom. Already in the late first century, Pope Saint Clement I (r. ca. 88–ca. 97) wrote about the problem of mixing genres when he prohibited the singing of liturgical music in secular surroundings.

> In the pagan festivals, let us not sing the psalms, and let us not read the Scriptures, for fear of seeming like the wandering

---

3   Edith Hamilton and Huntington Cairns, eds., *The Collected Dialogues of Plato Including the Letters* (New York: Pantheon Books, 1961), 1294–95.

minstrels, singers and tellers of tales of high adventure, who perform their art for a mouthful of bread. It is not fitting that we sing the canticles of the Lord in a strange land.[4]

Echoes of Pythagoras and Plato can be found in the writings of another Clement, Saint Clement of Alexandria (ca. 150–ca. 215). In his *Protrepticus*, Clement describes how the "New Song"—Christ, the Word—controls cosmic music, in contrast to pagan myths such as those of Orpheus and Amphion, who also evidenced the power of music.

> [The New Song] ordered the universe concordantly and tuned the discord of the elements in an harmonious arrangement, so that the entire cosmos might become through its agency a consonance. It let loose the rolling sea, yet checked it from advancing upon the earth. It stabilized the receding earth and established it as boundary to the sea. And indeed it even softened the raging fire with air as if tempering the Dorian harmony with the Lydian.[5]

The most influential conduit of the ancients' philosophy on music to Christian culture was Ancius Manlius Severinus Boethius (ca. 480–ca. 524). Best known for his *Consolation of Philosophy*, Boethius also left an unfinished book on music, *De institutione musica* (On the Instruction of Music). This became, as it were, the standard music theory textbook throughout the Middle Ages, and it enjoyed a revered status in later eras as well. In the beginning of Book 1, Boethius discusses the ethical dimension of music and cites Plato's Pythagorean-influenced dictum that "the soul of the universe was composed according

---

4   J.P. Migne, ed., *Patrologiae cursus completus: Patrologiae Graecae*, 167 vols. (Paris: J.P. Migne, 1844–1855), I, p. 432, trans. Robert Hayburn, quoted in Hayburn, *Papal Legislation on Sacred Music: 95 A.D. to 1977 A.D.* (Harrison, NY: Roman Catholic Books, 2005), 2.
5   *Protrepticus* I, 5, 1, trans. James McKinnon, in James McKinnon, ed., *Music in Early Christian Literature* (Cambridge: Cambridge University Press, 1988), p. 30.

to a musical harmony."[6] Boethius reviews Plato's teaching on the modes in the education of youth and relates stories concerning the power of music. Chapter 2 covers *musica mundana, musica humana,* and a third type of music—that which we actually hear—*musica instrumentalis.* In Chapter 10, Boethius retells the story of Pythagoras and the hammers; Chapters 11–33 are taken up with a presentation on ancient Greek music theory. In Chapter 34, Boethius defines the true Musician not as a practical musician, but as a philosopher—a man who studies and judges music. Book 2 of *De institutione musica* has just two chapters and ends with a definition of philosophy according to Pythagoras as "zeal for wisdom."

In a General Audience of March 12, 2008, Pope Benedict XVI discoursed on Boethius and his contemporary Cassiodorus (485–580). The Holy Father characterized Boethius as one who

> wrote manuals on arithmetic, geometry, music and astronomy, all with the intention of passing on the great Greco-Roman culture to the new generations, to the new times. In this context, in his commitment to fostering the encounter of cultures, he used the categories of Greek philosophy to present the Christian faith, here too seeking a synthesis between the Hellenistic-Roman heritage and the Gospel message. For this very reason Boethius was described as the last representative of ancient Roman culture and the first of the Medieval intellectuals.

These early writers illustrate the synthesis of ancient Greek philosophy with Christianity and, moreover, their consideration of the special place of music. In fact, music became a regular part of the *quadrivium,* the mathematical arts of the seven liberal arts.

---

6   Boethius, *Five Books on Music,* trans. James Garceau et al. (Self-published, 1985), 130.

2

Gregorian Chant:
Foundation of All Western Music

To claim that Gregorian chant is the foundation of all Western music may seem preposterous, but I hope to illustrate the truth of this. Even in secular universities and music conservatories, music majors must learn about chant's foundational role in Western music. John Senior has asked the question: "What is Christian Culture? . . . Christendom, what secularists call Western Civilization, is the Mass and the paraphernalia which protect and facilitate it."[1] Among the "paraphernalia" is music. Therefore, it is essential that Catholics become familiar with each musical element of Holy Mass. William Mahrt has noted that although liturgical scholars have done valuable work, "yet in studying the texts of the liturgy, some have forgotten that while liturgy is regulated largely in its texts, it does not consist of a series of texts to be read, but rather a series of sacred actions to be done."[2] And these sacred actions are sung; yes, every part of the Mass (except the sermon) was sung and can still be sung (even in the vernacular). So, let us begin our journey into Holy Mass, focusing particularly on its Proper chants.[3]

---

1   John Senior, *The Restoration of Christian Culture* (San Francisco: Ignatius Press, 1983), 15–16.

2   William Peter Mahrt, *The Musical Shape of the Liturgy* (Richmond: Church Music Association of America, 2012), 5.

3   Throughout this book, "Mass" refers to the Traditional Latin Mass, also known as the Extraordinary Form.

Following ancient cultures, Gregorian chant is monophonic and there are several ways to classify chant, but one is by text setting. The simplest kinds of chants, sung by everyone (priest, choir, and congregation), have texts set mainly syllabically, that is, one note of melody for each syllable of text. Examples are dialogues between celebrant and faithful (e.g., *Dominus vobiscum . . . Et cum spiritu tuo*) and Credo III,[4] which is widely sung. Spiritually, syllabic chants symbolize a proclamation or a paragraph; the Credo is a proclamation of faith, and we focus on whole paragraphs rather than dwelling on a word. The second type of text setting is neumatic—or semi-ornate—and can be described as anywhere from two to eight notes per syllable of text. One type of neumatic chant is the Communion antiphon, about which we will learn more shortly. Because neumatic chants have several notes of chant per syllable of text, the chant is more flowing, thus assuming a more contemplative aspect. The third type of text setting is melismatic—or ornate—in which there are anywhere from nine to fifty-plus notes per syllable of text. This is the most contemplative type of chant; one example is the Alleluia before the Gospel. Another way to classify Gregorian chants is through consideration of the modes. Modes are the building blocks of chant; they are special scales and melodic patterns. For our purposes, I shall focus on the *ethos*—or character—of each mode instead of discussing modal theory. Aside from the celebrant's prayers and the priest-faithful dialogues, the Mass prayers fall into two groups: Ordinary and Proper. The Ordinary texts are those that are unchanging from Mass to Mass—Kyrie,

---

4   The Roman numeral refers to the numbering in Vatican editions of Gregorian chant. Each set of Ordinary chants (Kyrie, Gloria, Sanctus, Agnus Dei), totaling eighteen, is given a number. The Credo, which was the last prayer/chant to be added to the Mass, is in a separate section; there are only six Credos in the Vatican edition.

Gloria, Credo, Sanctus, Agnus Dei, and Ite missa est. Ordinary chants can often be sung by the faithful.

The Proper texts are those that change with each Mass, and these texts, with their melodies, are making a comeback after having practically vanished post-Vatican II. Most Proper texts come from Holy Scripture—especially the psalms—and commonly consist of the Introit, Gradual, Alleluia, Offertory, and Communion.[5] In the early Church the Fathers elucidated not only the words of Christ in the Gospels but also the whole of Scripture, both Old and New Testaments. The Christological biblical exegeses of Saints John Chrysostom, Ambrose, Jerome, Augustine, and others were read and appreciated, but the wider community of the faithful became familiar with these interpretations through the chanted Mass.

The Proper chants for the Midnight Mass are about the identity of Christ, the eternal Logos who is now being born of the Father. Saint Augustine will interpret these chants for us. The Introit text is taken from Psalm 2 and the melody is Mode 2. Certain writers described the *ethos* of Mode 2 as "deep-voiced seriousness" and "agreeable."

Antiphon: Psalm 2:7

Dóminus dixit ad me: Fílius meus es tu, ego hódie génui te.	The Lord hath said to Me: Thou art My Son, this day have I begotten Thee.

Verse: Psalm 2:1

Quare fremuérunt gentes: et pópuli meditáti sunt inánia?	Why have the Gentiles raged and the people devised vain things?

---

5   Starting with the pre-Lent Sunday of Septuagesima (the third Sunday before Lent), the Alleluia is replaced by a chant called the Tract, and during Eastertide there are two Alleluias, instead of a Gradual and an Alleluia.

Doxology

V. Glória Patri, et Fílio, et Spirítui Sancto.	V. Glory be to the Father, and to the Son, and to the Holy Ghost.
R. Sicut erat in princípio, et nunc, et semper, et in sǽcula sæculórum. Amen.	R. As it was in the beginning, is now, and ever shall be, world without end. Amen.

Repeat Antiphon.

Saint Augustine, in his *Commentary on the Psalms*, offers this interpretation of verse 7, which is used both in the Introit and in the Proper verse of the Alleluia:

> Although that day may also seem to be prophetically spoken of, on which Jesus Christ was born according to the flesh; and in eternity there is nothing past as if it had ceased to be, nor future as if it were not yet, but present only, since whatever is eternal, always is; yet as today intimates presentiality, a divine interpretation is given to that expression, "Today have I begotten Thee," whereby the uncorrupt and Catholic faith proclaims the eternal generation of the power and Wisdom of God, who is the Only-begotten Son.[6]

Of the psalm's verse 1, the beginning of the Introit's verse, Augustine observes:

> It is said, "why?" as if it were said, in vain. For what they wished, namely, Christ's destruction, they accomplished not; for this is spoken of our Lord's persecutors, of whom also mention is made in the Acts of the Apostles (Acts 4:26).[7]

---

6   Augustine, *Expositions on the Book of Psalms*, trans. A. Cleveland Coxe, https://www.ccel.org/ccel/schaff/npnf108.ii.II_1.html.
7   Ibid.

The Introit's musical form is seen in the above translation. The antiphon is a melody that is normally in neumatic style. The verse and Doxology are set to a psalm tone, a syllabic melodic formula for chanting the psalms.

The Gradual is chanted after the Epistle (first reading).[8] It is one of two Proper chants, along with the Alleluia, that are always melismatic and thus more contemplative.[9] The Gradual and Alleluia are also contemplative because of their location between the Epistle and Gospel, a good place for meditation on the Scriptures. The text of the Respond (first half of the Gradual) is drawn from Psalm 110 (109), another Christological psalm. Like the Introit, the Gradual is also a Mode 2 melody.

Respond: Psalm 110 (109):3

Tecum princípium in die virtútis tuæ: in splendóribus sanctórum, ex útero ante lucíferum génui te.	With Thee is the beginning in the day of Thy strength: in the brightness of the Saints: from the womb before the day star I begot Thee.

Verse: Psalm 110 (109):1

Dixit Dóminus Dómino meo: Sede a dextris meis: donec ponam inimícos tuos, scabéllum pedum tuórum.	The Lord said to my Lord: Sit Thou at My right hand: Until I make Thy enemies Thy footstool.

The text of the Gradual's verse is the beginning of Psalm 110 (109); Saint Augustine indicates the Christological nature of Psalm 110 (109) by reminding us that verse 1 was quoted by Jesus in Matthew 22:42–45 when He asks the Jews, Whose

---

8   In the *Novus ordo* Mass, the Gradual is usually replaced by the responsorial psalm.
9   In both the Gradual and Alleluia, I have indicated the most melismatic syllables below with boldface.

son is the Christ? He answers that Christ is both David's Son and David's Lord.

Saint Augustine discusses this at the beginning of his commentary, but in paragraph 4, he references Psalm 2:1 ("Why do the heathen ..."), which was also used for the Introit verse, and Psalm 110 (109):3, which is used for the Respond. Augustine has woven a rich cloth of prophetic scriptural references that can resonate with us as we sing or listen to this Gradual.

The Alleluia is a Mode 8 chant and its Proper verse repeats the text of the Introit antiphon. The melody is the same as that used for—among other Masses—the First Sunday of Advent, thus emphasizing the mode's *ethos*, which some medieval writers describe as "joyful or exultant."

Alleluia, alleluia.	Alleluia.
Verse: Psalm 2:7	
Dóminus dixit ad me: Fílius meus es tu, ego hódie génui te.	The Lord said to Me, Thou art My Son; this day I have begotten Thee.
Alleluia.	Alleluia.

Scholars have written of the syllable "-ia" in the Alleluia, calling it the *jubilus* because of its wordless expression of jubilation. Saint Augustine, in his commentary on Psalm 94, describes this phenomenon.

> It is a certain sound of joy without words, the expression of a mind poured forth in joy. A man rejoicing in his own exultation, after certain words which cannot be understood, bursteth forth into sounds of exultation without words, so that it seemeth that he, filled with excessive joy, cannot express in words the subject of that joy.[10]

---

10   Gustave Reese, *Music in the Middle Ages* (New York: W. W. Norton, 1940), 164.

The Offertory is a Mode 4 chant whose *ethos* is described as "adulatory," "moderate," "serious," or "lingering." It announces that the Lord is coming and that all nature should rejoice. Verses of this psalm also appear in the Mass of Christmas Day. Offertory chants tend to be melismatic but this one is more neumatic and quite short.

Psalm 96 (95):11, 13

Læténtur cæli, et exsúltet terra ante fáciem Dómini: quóniam venit.	Let the heavens rejoice, and let the earth be glad before the face of the Lord: because He cometh.

The Communion antiphon is a Mode 6 chant, and the text repeats part of the Respond (first half) of the Gradual chant. Some medieval theorists label the *ethos* of Mode 6 as "mournful," "voluptuous," and "lachrymose." Certainly, the text of this chant is not "mournful" or "lachrymose," but since it is a restatement of the psalm verse used in the Gradual and because it refers to the mystery of God made man, one could think of this as a joyful, yet deeply serious chant. Again, the text setting is neumatic and the chant is quite short.

Psalm 110 (109):3

In splendóribus sanctórum, ex útero ante lucíferum génui te.	In the brightness of the Saints, from the womb before the day star I begot Thee.

Gregorian chant is a totally humble art that also happens to be sublime prayer. There is no other reason for which it was composed than the praise of God.

3

Illuminations:
The Century of Saint Hildegard of Bingen

The medievals had a penchant for embellishment in almost every aspect of life—social ritual, scholarly commentary (glosses, aka annotations), the writing of chronicles, and the illumination of manuscripts. Moreover, the liturgy was embellished with new saints' days, and all of these required new chants for the Mass and Office. The Proper texts were drawn from biblical references—direct and indirect—to the Blessed Virgin or from the *vitæ* (lives of the saints), as well as Scripture that could be accommodated to the saints. The eleventh century saw the institution of the Saturday Lady Mass and also the seasonal Marian antiphons—*Alma Redemptoris Mater*, *Ave Regina cælorum*, *Regina cæli*, and *Salve Regina*.

Other embellishments extended to liturgical chant in the form of tropes. These tropes were either additions of words and music to an existing chant, additions of words alone to an existing chant (*prosula*), or the addition of a wordless melisma to an existing chant. These tropes, or embellishments, can be considered as glosses (commentaries) on the chant. Just as the Church Fathers commented on Sacred Scripture—as we saw with Saint Augustine's commentary on Psalms 2 and 110 (109)—so the medieval musicians glossed, or commented on, the chants, both Ordinary and Proper, and some chants of the Divine Office.

Sometimes the trope was a complete entity, placed before the chant it was embellishing, as in *Quem quæritis in sepulchro?*

(Whom do you seek in the tomb?), a dialogue between the Angel and the Three Women (Marys) that was sung before the Introit for Easter Sunday. At other times the added text and melody were interpolated between sections of the "parent" chant, as in a trope of the first part (antiphon) of *Resurrexi*, the Introit for Easter Sunday. In the English translation below, the troped text is indicated by italics.

> *Rejoice and be glad, because the Lord is risen, Alleluia.*
> *Let us rejoice in Him, saying, Eia, Alleluia.*
> I am risen,
> *When God arose in judgment*
> And I am still with thee, alleluia:
> *The earth trembled, when Christ arose from the dead,*
> Thou hast laid Thy hand upon me, alleluia:
> *There was made a great earthquake, the angel of the Lord*
>   *descended from heaven,*
> Wonderful has become
> *The guards became as dead men*
> Thy knowledge
> *For great fear of the angels,*
> Alleluia, alleluia.

The third and fourth troped lines refer not only to Psalm 76 (75):9, 10, but also to the Offertory antiphon, *Terra tremuit* (The earth trembled), which uses this psalm in another instance of a Christological accommodation of the Old Testament. And, of course, the Offertory antiphon is a reference to Matthew 28:2, when an earthquake heralds the descent of the angel, who rolls back the stone on Christ's tomb at the Resurrection.

In the ninth century the Sequence, another new genre of liturgical chant, arose; possibly it began as a *prosula*, the addition of words to a melismatic section of chant, like the *jubilus* of the Alleluia. In fact, the sequence was traditionally sung after the Alleluia; the addition of words to the melismatic *jubilus*, then, transformed a melismatic chant into a new syllabic chant. Sequences soon began to be composed as autonomous chants and were very popular in the tenth to thirteenth centuries and beyond. Most sequences, however, were excised from the Mass at the Council of Trent. This left only four, which are still sung today; they are *Victimæ paschali laudes* (Easter), *Veni Sancte Spiritus* (Pentecost), *Lauda Sion* (Corpus Christi), and *Dies iræ* (Requiem Mass). *Stabat mater* (*At the cross her station keeping*) was restored in 1727 and assigned to the Feast of the Seven Dolors of Our Lady (September 15). Most readers will know it, however, from its popular use during Lenten Stations of the Cross.

Liturgical drama is the last new chant genre that we shall mention. Its ancestor is the trope, for example, *Quem quæritis*, described above. The fact that such tropes were dialogues naturally suggested an acting out of the words, and so *Quem quæritis* and other tropes began to be acted inside or outside of churches. Eventually, tropes grew in length and then became autonomous from the liturgy. A good example of a liturgical drama is *Ludus Danielis* (*The Play of Daniel*), which was first revived and recorded in the 1950s.

On October 7, 2012, Pope Benedict XVI proclaimed the twelfth-century Benedictine abbess Hildegard of Bingen (1098–1179) a Doctor of the Church and a saint of the Roman calendar. Hildegard had already been recognized in the Benedictine calendar as a saint for many centuries, but now the pope elevated her to the universal, Roman calendar.

Saint Hildegard was the tenth child of Hildebert and Mechtild of Bermersheim, a noble couple. When she was eight years old, her parents tithed her to the anchoress Jutta von Spanheim, who lived in a cell attached to the Benedictine monastery of Disibodenberg. Jutta, a very young woman from another noble family in the area, taught Hildegard how to read the Scriptures in Latin, how to chant the Divine Office, and other aspects of religious life. On All Saints' Day 1112, Jutta and Hildegard made their vows as Benedictine nuns before Bishop Otto of Bamberg. Gradually, their hermitage developed into a Benedictine community of nuns, as other girls from noble families in the area were drawn to the vowed life lived by Jutta and Hildegard. In 1136, at Jutta's death, Hildegard was appointed prioress of the community, which was under the care of the abbot of Disibodenberg.

Five years later Hildegard received a vision of "tongues of flame" and a "divine call" to write down the visions that she had been having since about the age of five. She had been too afraid to reveal the visions to anyone but Jutta, the abbot Disibodenberg, and the monk Volmar, who became the scribe of these visions after the abbot encouraged her to record them. Up to her forty-third year, Hildegard had lived an undocumented, seemingly ordinary life of a Benedictine nun, but now she began a new life as prophetess, poet, and composer. Around 1146 or 1147 she wrote to the abbot of Clairvaux, the future Saint Bernard, to seek his counsel about her visions; Bernard replied briefly and encouragingly. Bernard's endorsement of Hildegard's visions was to bear even more fruit when Pope Eugenius III, a Cistercian monk and a student of Bernard, happened to hear about her during a bishops' synod that was held at Trier, not far from Hildegard's monastery. Bernard was with the pope in Trier and had informed him about Hildegard. After having Hildegard's writings brought to him from the monastery, Eugenius read them and sent her a letter with his apostolic blessing. Now that she had the pope's approval and protection, Hildegard became something of a celebrity throughout Europe. Her advice was sought by people of all stations of life, including even the emperor, Friedrich Barbarossa.

One letter of many Hildegard received was from Odo of Soissons, master of theology at the University of Paris. Odo wrote: "It is reported that, exalted, you see many things in the heavens and record them in your writing, and that you bring forth the melody of a new song, although you have studied nothing of such things."[1] Fourteen of these songs would be included in *Scivias*, Hildegard's first "book," completed in 1151, after ten years of recording the visions. The *Scivias* is an abbreviated version of the work's title, *Sci vias Domini* (*Know the Ways of the Lord*).

The fourteen songs in *Scivias* are not the only music Hildegard composed, for all during this latter part of her life she was composing poetry and songs that have come down to us in two manuscripts. The total number of notated musical works is seventy-seven, and many bear the names of various genres of liturgical music—antiphons, responses, sequences, and hymns. There are also a Kyrie, an Alleluia, and three songs that are unlabeled. Modern scholars have dubbed the collected songs *Symphonia armoniae celestium revelationum* (*Symphony of the Harmony of Celestial Revelations*). Most of these songs—or chants, actually—would have found a place in the liturgies at Hildegard's monastery. In addition to melodies in praise of the Blessed Trinity, Hildegard composed both lyrics and melodies that would complement the Commons of the Blessed Virgin Mary, the Apostles, Martyrs, Confessors (Bishops), and Virgins, as well as chants to honor angels, patriarchs, and prophets. Some of the chants honored local patron saints such as Saints Eucharius and Maximinus (early bishops of Trier), Saint Disibodus (patron of Disibodenberg

---

1   "Odo of Soissons to Hildegard, 1148–49 (?)", in *The Letters of Hildegard of Bingen*, vol. 1, trans. Joseph L. Baird & Radd K. Ehrman (New York/Oxford: Oxford University Press, 1994), 110.

monastery), and Saint Ursula and her eleven thousand virgin companions, martyred at Cologne.

Another masterpiece of Hildegard's is *Ordo virtutum*, which many see as the first morality play. It includes eighty-two melodies, and concerns the rescue of the soul, *Anima*, from the devil by sixteen personified virtues. All of the characters except *Diabolus* sing; indeed, he shouts his lines, which brings to mind Lorenzo's caution to Jessica in *The Merchant of Venice* that "the man that hath no music in him ... let no such man be trusted."[2] Both Shakespeare and Hildegard were heirs to the same musical aesthetic originating in Pythagoras and Plato, and transmitted through Aristotle, Augustine, and Boethius. This was the idea that music, with its acoustical system of intervals mathematically ordered by ratios, mirrors the organization of the cosmos. In the apocalyptic thirteenth vision from *Scivias*, Hildegard acknowledges the Trinitarian aspect of music: "And so the words symbolize the body, and the jubilant music indicates the spirit; and the celestial harmony shows the Divinity, and the words the Humanity of the Son of God."[3] Hildegard clearly viewed music as a gift of God, that like the Holy Spirit, vivifies us and brings us closer to Him.

Like much other twelfth-century music, Hildegard's is monophonic. Her melodies will remind the listener somewhat of Gregorian chant, and yet because of their unique style, many of the melodies sound soaring and ecstatic. Very often the range of Hildegard's melodies span an octave and a fourth or fifth, exceeding that of the typical Gregorian chant. One example would be *Alleluia. O virga mediatrix* (*Alleluia.*

---

2   William Shakespeare, *The Merchant of Venice*, ed. Joseph Pearce, Ignatius Critical Editions (San Francisco: Ignatius Press, 2009), 5.1.83–87. (Numerals refer to act, scene, and lines.)

3   Cf. *Scivias* 3,13,12, *Hildegard of Bingen: Scivias*, trans. Columba Hart and Jane Bishop (New York: Paulist Press, 1990), 533.

O mediating branch). This is a Gospel Alleluia with a verse honoring the Blessed Virgin.

Alleluia!	Alleluia!
O virga mediatrix,	O branch and mediatrix,
sancta viscera tua	your sacred flesh
mortem superaverunt	has conquered death,
et venter tuus omnes creaturas	your womb all creatures
illuminavit	illumined
in pulchro flore de suavissima	in beauty's bloom from that
integritate	exquisite purity
clausi pudoris tui	of your enclosèd modesty
orto.	sprung forth.

In the last twenty years this holy Benedictine abbess has emerged from centuries of obscurity, and there is a burgeoning bibliography and discography of her works. However, there has been a measure of distortion concerning Hildegard's life, motives, and philosophy, as different interest groups have discovered Hildegard and adapted elements of her writings to fit their agendas. Even though Hildegard was a faithful Catholic who understood our need for salvation through Christ, Matthew Fox—formerly a Dominican priest and now an Episcopalian clergyman—has hailed her as a proto-theologian of his "creation spirituality." Feminists, too, see in Hildegard an early champion of women's rights, for example, standing up to men who were perceived as hindering her from achieving her goals, as when she started her own monastery at Rupertsberg on the Rhine at Bingen.

Like Saint Teresa of Ávila, who weathered the storms of life while experiencing and writing about her mystical union with God, Hildegard of Bingen also lived a full and active life—full of struggles and conflicts—while writing poems of ecstatic joy and praise. To read Hildegard's own writing and to listen to her music is to get a more complete picture of this remarkable woman and to see what great love she had for Christ and His Church.

4

Knights, Troubadours, and Pilgrims

Alongside the vast treasury of Gregorian chant that was composed—and written down after the ninth-century advent of musical notation—a repertory of secular song began to develop. The first body of vernacular secular poetry and melodies consists of tales of knightly honor and courtly love. Many of the poets themselves were knights, and their poems typified the fusion of chivalry with romantic love, a concept that has lasted even to today. The great Catholic historian Christopher Dawson has written in *Religion and the Rise of Western Culture* that

> the gradual leavening of the heroic ethos by the influence of the Church finds its literary expression in the *chansons de geste,* which represent the authentic spirit of feudal society in contrast to the romantic poetry of the troubadours and the courtly epic, which seem to belong to an entirely different world.... For the age of the Crusades also saw the development of a new secular ideal of chivalry which seems the direct antithesis of St. Bernard's ideal of Christian Knighthood and the disciplined austerity of the Military Orders, while at the same time it was equally remote from the barbaric heroism of Northern feudalism. This new ideal is the creation of the South.[1]

---

1   Christopher Dawson, *Religion and the Rise of Western Culture* (New York: Image Books, 1958), 152.

This new culture of romantic love arose, seemingly spon-
taneously, in the duchy of Aquitaine, located in the south-
central region of modern-day France, and it subsequently
spread to other areas. The dukes of Aquitaine were powerful
and were not subsumed into the French kingdom until the
fifteenth century. The twelfth century saw a flourishing of
Aquitanian culture, not only because of the dukes of Aquitaine but also because of the presence of the Abbey of Saint
Martial (Limoges), a stopping-place for pilgrims on the way to
Santiago de Compostela.

The earliest known writer of European vernacular poetry
was indeed a knight. He was William (Guillaume, or Guil-
hem), seventh Count of Poitiers and ninth Duke of Aquitaine
(1071–ca. 1127); he is also renowned for being the grandfa-
ther of Eleanor (Aliénor) of Aquitaine (1122–1204). Eleanor
herself played a role in the story of the troubadour song, as we
shall see. Eleven of William's lyric poems survive, though only
one has a melody, and that is not complete.

The troubadours were the "poet-composers" whose name
comes from *trobar*, the Provençal verb meaning literally "to
find," but by extension "to compose a song." Provençal is a
dialect of Occitan, or Langue d'oc, the language of south-
eastern France. These poet-composers were men (and some
women) of various states in life, but many were knights.

How do we know anything at all about the troubadours?
We can glean some information about their lives from their
poems, from the *razos* (introductions to their songs found
in the chansonniers—or manuscripts—of their songs), and
from the *vidas*, biographies (lives) of the troubadours, that are
found in manuscripts. One of the most famous of the troubadours was Bernart (or Bernatz) de Ventadorn (ca. 1140–
ca. 1190). His biographer, Hugh (Uc) of Saint-Circ, tells
us that Bernart's parents were servants at the chateau of the
Count of Ventadorn, Eble III. Hugh tells us that God blessed

Bernart with good looks and poetic and musical talent, so much so that Marguerite de Turenne, the wife of Count Eble fell in love with the troubadour. Eventually the count dismissed Bernart and he went north to Normandy, where he entered the service of the Duke of Normandy, Henry Plantagenet, and his wife, Eleanor of Aquitaine. Bernart fell in love with Eleanor, and she with him, but they were parted when the duke became King Henry II of England. From Normandy, Bernart returned south and attached himself to the court of Count Raymond VI of Toulouse, and after the death of the count, Bernart retired to the Cistercian Abbey of Dalon, where he lived as a penitent for his remaining years.

A famous example of Bernart's art is his *canso* entitled *Can vei la lauzeta mover* (When I see the lark moving). The first two stanzas of the poem broach a troubadour's common plaint, his rejection by the lady he adores.

When I see the lark moving
Its wings joyfully against the
   rays of the sun,
And then abandon itself and
   let itself fall
Because of the bliss in its
   heart,
Oh! Such envy do I feel
For those that are happy,
That I am amazed that my
   heart does not
Instantly melt with longing.

Alas! I thought I knew so
   much about
Love, but know in truth so
   little,
For I cannot help myself
   loving
One who gives me nothing in
   return.
My whole heart, myself,
Herself, and the whole world
She has taken from me, and
   left me nothing
But desire and a yearning
   heart.

The era of the troubadours coincided with the expansion of veneration given to the Blessed Virgin Mary. One of the main advocates was Saint Bernard of Clairvaux (1090–1153), who preached and wrote extensively and mellifluously (*Doctor mellifluus*) on our Lady.

As exemplars of poets writing distinguished vernacular poetry, the troubadours inspired Dante in his own development as a poet. Among those whose works he quotes in his treatise on vernacular poetry *De vulgari eloquentia* (On vernacular eloquence) are Bertran de Born, Arnaut Daniel, and Folquet of Marseilles. These three are worth mentioning, not only for their music and lyrics but also because Dante included them in the three different realms of the *Commedia*.

We meet Bertran de Born (ca. 1145–1215) in Canto XXVIII of the *Inferno*, where Dante portrays him carrying his own severed head, punishment for stirring up strife between Henry II and Henry's son. Bertran was a military man of noble lineage who ultimately entered a Cistercian monastery for about the last twenty years of his life. Only one of his forty or so poems has survived with his own melody. This is the *sirventes* (a "song of service" to a noble lord), *Rassa, tan creis e monta e poia* (Rassa, who increases and mounts). Although Bertran is a poet and musician, Dante's Hell is notable for the general absence of music. More characteristic are "sighs, plaints, and deep wailings ... strange tongues, horrible outcries, words of pain, tones of anger, voices deep and hoarse" ("sospiri, pianti, e alti guai ... diverse lingue, orribili favelle, parole di dolore, accenti d'ira, voci alti e fioche" [Canto III, 22–30]).

In Purgatory Dante encounters one of his most admired troubadour poets, Arnaut Daniel (ca. 1150–ca. 1200). Although Dante deems Arnaut the poet of love in *De vulgari eloquentia* and "best of all" in the *Commedia*, he also includes him in Canto XXVI of *Purgatorio*, in Cornice VII, among the lustful. Two of Arnaut's melodies survive with his eighteen poems; they are *Lo ferm qu'el cor m'intra* (The strong will which enters my heart) and *Chanson do'ill mot son plan e prim* (I will make a song plain and prime).

In Canto IX we meet the troubadour that Dante placed in Heaven. Folquet of Marseilles (ca. 1155–1231) was a renowned troubadour for whom we have twenty-nine poems, thirteen of which have melodies. Two of them are *Tant m'abellis l'amoros pessamens* (So pleasing to me is the amorous thought) and *Ben an mort* (Themselves and me they've brought to death). After living the worldly life of a troubadour from about 1180, Folquet experienced a radical conversion and in 1195 entered the Cistercian order. In the next phase of his life, he was abbot of Thoronet abbey from about 1201 and then became bishop of Toulouse in about 1205. It was here that Bishop Folquet met Dominic de Guzman and joined forces with him in combating the Albigensian heresy. Bishop Folquet was instrumental in helping Saint Dominic found the Order of Preachers.

Pilgrimage was a major phenomenon of the Middle Ages, with the Holy Land and Rome topping the list of most visited sites. The third most popular pilgrimage site, however, was Santiago de Compostela, whose cathedral contains the relics of Saint James the Greater. Housed in the cathedral library is a late thirteenth-century manuscript known as the *Liber Sancti Jacobi* (The Book of Saint James), which contains a "guidebook" for pilgrims, the complete orders of worship—and plainchant—for both the Vigil and the Feast of Saint James, and a collection of polyphonic songs for two or three voices. This amazing liturgical and extra-liturgical music in the *Book of Saint James* was meant to be sung not by pilgrims, but by clerics or trained musicians. There are no remaining popular pilgrim songs specifically related to the pilgrimage to Compostela, so we can only dream about what pilgrims might have sung while on the Camino Real.

There is another pilgrimage site, however, which does have a small collection of pilgrim songs. After the shrine of Santiago de Compostela, probably no other Spanish pilgrimage site was as revered and popular as the shrine of Our Lady of Montserrat, where even today pilgrims flock to the Benedictine abbey to view the miraculous Black Virgin of Montserrat statue.

One of the treasures of the library at Abadia Montserrat is the *Llibre vermell,* or "The Red Book." This manuscript was compiled at the end of the fourteenth century and providentially escaped total destruction when the monastery was burned in 1811 during the War of Spanish Independence. At some point in the nineteenth century, the leaves were gathered and bound in a book covered in red velvet, hence the name *Llibre vermell* (think "vermilion"). The bulk of the *Llibre vermell* contains devotional writings, but interspersed among them are about ten songs. The manuscript itself contains a key to the use of the songs; the anonymous scribe wrote after the first song in red lettering—in the manner of rubrics—that

> pilgrims sometimes wish to sing and dance while keeping their night vigil in the church of Our Lady of Montserrat, and also during the day-time on the square in front of the church. Only righteous and pious songs may be sung in here; to this end the songs will be designated with indications above and below them. They must be performed in a respectful and sober manner, so as not to disturb those praying, or the contemplation of pious folk; all present should behave in a seemly fashion and a pious spirit.[2]

The "chaste and pious" songs, with one exception, are all in praise of the Blessed Virgin, and five of them are types of

---

2   John Sidgwick, trans., *Liner Notes to Llibre Vermell de Montserrat, Cantigas de Santa Maria* (Alla Francesca, voix et instruments du Moyen Age), Opus 111 OPS 30–131 (1995), 18.

dance songs. Also included are three canons—or rounds—and two polyphonic songs, one for two voices and one for three voices.

Performers of medieval music must exercise creativity because, in general, manuscripts of medieval music show only one melodic line and give no indication of what voice or instrument should perform it. Thus, it is up to the performer to decide how to realize the music, in order to present it compellingly to a modern audience. The first song, *O Virgo splendens* (O shining Virgin), is an intricate and somewhat melismatic canon for three voices. The lyrics begin: "O Virgo / Splendens hic in **monte** celso / Miraculis **serrato**" (O Virgin / shining over this lofty mountain / set with miracles), thus making a direct reference to Montserrat. The brief poem refers also to the pilgrims who come to the mountain and ask the intercession of the Holy Virgin.

While most of the songs in the *Llibre vermell* are in Latin, some are in the vernacular. For instance, the refrain of *Los set goytx* (The seven joys) is in Latin and the verses are in Catalan and recount the seven joys of Mary. These are the traditional seven joys that are almost a commonplace of medieval literature: (1) the Annunciation, (2) Christ's Nativity, (3) the Adoration of the Three Kings, (4) the Resurrection, (5) the Ascension, (6) Pentecost, and (7) the Coronation of Our Lady.

Finally, "Media vita in morte sumus" (In the midst of life we are in death). That is not the title of the final song, but it could be, as this series of paeans to the Virgin of Montserrat ends with "Ad mortem festinamus" (We hurry toward death), an exhortation to the pilgrims to give up sin and convert. The monk who assembled these songs had the care of souls in mind as he provided songs for the pilgrims' use in the fourteenth century, but the songs of the *Llibre vermell* remain for us to sing and pray in the twenty-first century. *Ave Maria!*

5

Polyphony: Building a Cathedral in Music

As long as people have been singing, there has probably always been a fancy to "harmonize," or add another voice to a melody. However, the written record of history does not mention polyphony until the ninth century.

The ninth is also the century that furnishes the first written evidence of two-voice polyphony; these are some short examples of parallel organum, in which an added voice moves below a Gregorian chant melody in parallel movement, at the interval of a fourth or a fifth (i.e., a distance of four notes or five notes below the chant melody). These examples exist in the *Musica enchiriadis* (Music handbook), a medieval music theory book from the late 800s.[1] It describes this parallel organum as *diaphonia* (diaphony, "singing together"). One of these examples is a snippet from the hymn *Te Deum laudamus* (We praise Thee, o God), and we can see that this is just another manifestation of the medieval penchant for embellishment— one could call it a *vertical trope*. The term "organum" can mean more than one thing in medieval sources, but for our purposes we shall limit it to a general term for all chant-based polyphonic music up to around 1250. Parallel organum was relatively short-lived, as variety is the spice of life for composers, and so other types of movement—oblique, contrary— between the two voices began to be employed in organum.

---

1   Claude Palisca, ed., and Raymond Erickson, trans., *Musica enchiriadis and Scolica enchiriadis* (New Haven: Yale University Press, 1995).

The foundation of organum is Gregorian chant, the consummate Christian music, just as the foundation of a medieval church or cathedral is usually cross-shaped. And if one were to continue the analogy with architecture, monophonic Gregorian chant could be compared to an early Roman Christian basilica. The added parallel voice (*vox organalis*) was "troped" above the chant (*vox principalis*) on account of the liturgical importance of the chant.

The Old Minster—Winchester Cathedral before the new, Norman cathedral was consecrated in 1093—was the *locus* of the largest manuscript of two-voice organa, compiled around the year 1000. This royal Anglo-Saxon cathedral was the resting place of Alfred the Great and a number of the earliest kings of Wessex. The Old Minster housed, in addition to the church, a priory of Benedictine monks and a pilgrimage site containing relics of Saint Swithun (d. 863), a former bishop of Winchester. This compact manuscript contains 164 two-voice settings of responsories for the night office of Matins, and would have been used by a precentor, whose duty was to lead the singing at Mass and the Divine Office.

Another way in which early polyphony could be considered a "vertical trope" is the way in which it was used in the liturgy. Typically, the execution of Gregorian chant was divided between the choir and the soloists, with cantors, or soloists, singing the first word(s)—the incipit—of each chant and then being responded to by the whole choir. In certain chants, for example, the Gradual and the Alleluia, there was a verse that was sung by the soloists. Thus, the earliest polyphony was an embellishment of the soloists' portions of the chant. The rest of a chant was sung by the full choir in its original—and easier— monophonic form, alternating with the sections in polyphony.

Let's see how this works in *Alleluia Justus ut palma* (Alleluia, the righteous like a palm tree [shall flourish]), a polyphonic Alleluia for two voices from about 1100, which comes from a treatise called *Ad organum faciendum* (How to make organum). This manuscript was the first to show the place-ment of the *vox principalis* (the chant) beneath—and not above—the *vox organalis* (the added voice). Now the chant—what Pope John XXII (r. 1316–1334) would call "the funda-mental sources of our melodies"—was somewhat obscured by the *vox organalis*, the added voice.

In *Alleluia Justus ut palma*, the relationship of the two voices to each other is mostly note-against-note and the motion between them is a mixture of parallel, oblique, and contrary. The proper Alleluia verse is from Psalm 92 (91):13 and is used for any Mass of a Holy Abbot. The table below summarizes the relationship between the Gregorian chant Alleluia and the sections of organum (polyphony). I have indicated the most melismatic syllables below with boldface.

Soloists	Choir	Soloists	Choir
Polyph.	Chant	Polyphony	Chant
Allelúia	Allelú**ia**	Justus ut palma florébit, et sicut **ce**drus	Multiplicá**bitur**

The just man shall flourish like the palm tree:
he shall grow up like the cedar of Lebanon.

This note-against-note style of organum duplum (i.e., for two voices) could be compared to either a Roman basilica or a Romanesque cathedral or church. Both have rounded arches, but the Romanesque church has a two-story elevation, with semi-circular arches above each rounded arch. In addition, a Romanesque church or cathedral usually displays a riot of many small decorations carved in stone.

In the twelfth century a new style of organum developed. Known as melismatic organum (or Aquitanian or florid or Saint Martial), it survives mainly in four manuscripts associated with the pilgrimage to Santiago de Compostela. One of them, the *Codex Callixtinus*, is actually from the monastery at Compostela and contains two-voice organa that are settings of Matins responsories.

Three manuscripts were once owned by the Abbey of St. Martial at Limoges in Aquitaine, in south-central France; this important monastery was a stopping-place on the route to Compostela. We see in these manuscripts that the lower voice—now called the *tenor*—was written in notes of longer values, the upper voice swirling above it as a florid, melismatic embellishment. Because of this florid upper voice (now called *duplum*), melismatic organum can be compared to a Romanesque church in which each of the rounded arches each have two smaller rounded arches above them, denoting a more decorative style. One example of melismatic organum associated with the Abbey of Saint Martial, Limoges, is *Jubilemus, exultemus*. It is a setting of a rhymed and metered festive poem (or *versus*) written to be sung at the end of Christmas Matins. Thus, while it is not liturgical music, per se, it is a trope on *Benedicamus Domino*.[2] *Jubilemus, exultemus* features the alternation between melismatic and note-against-note style, but no alternation between soloists and choir.

Jubilemus, exultemus,	Let us jubilate, exult,
intonemus canticum	let us intone our song
Redemptori, plasmatori	to the Redeemer, to the maker
Salvatori omnium!	to the Savior of all!
Hoc nathali salutari	In this lifegiving Christmas
omnis nostra turmula	let all our little host
Deum laudet, sibi plaudet	praise God and dance for him
per eterna secula.	through endless ages.

---

2   The words of dismissal from the Divine Office and from Masses in which the Gloria is not sung.

Qui hodie de Marie	Who, coming out today
utero progrediens,	from Mary's womb,
homo verus, rex et herus	appeared on earth true man
in terris apparuit.	and King and master.
Iam beatum ergo natum	Joining the praise and exultation
cum ingenti gaudio	at this blissful child,
conlaudantes exultantes,	with immense joy
Benedicamus Domino!	let us now bless the Lord!

After several more developments in polyphony, not to be recounted here, we reach the apex in what is known as Notre Dame polyphony. This style, associated with the cathedral of Our Lady of Paris (Notre-Dame de Paris), developed principally during the first forty years of the cathedral's construction, that is, from about 1160 to 1200. One eyewitness—perhaps a student or an instructor at the University of Paris from about 1225 until 1250—briefly described the music of the Notre Dame School and its two illustrious composers—Leoninus (1135–1201) and Perotinus (1160–1230). Earning his name because of his position in a group of anonymous medieval manuscripts that were published in 1864, Anonymous IV is the first writer to mention these—or any—composers by name. He tells us that Leoninus was the best composer of organum and that Magister Leoninus compiled a large book (*Magnus Liber*) of two-voice organa for the Divine Office and Mass, for the entire liturgical year. According to Anonymous IV, Perotinus "improved" the organum of Leoninus by substituting new sections (*clausulæ*) from his own compositions. Anonymous IV also tells us that Perotinus composed organa for three and four voices. These massive compositions are worth examining, so let us consider *Viderunt omnes*, the Gradual chant for the Mass of Christmas Day. Settings of this by both Leoninus and Perotinus remain. As described above, only the solo portions (incipit and verse) of the chant were set to polyphony; the rest of the chant was Gregorian chant sung by the whole choir. In the incipit—*Viderunt omnes*—of the organum, the original chant melody is set out in extremely long notes, and as usual by now, the chant is buried on the lowest vocal line, the tenor. Leoninus' setting is for two voices (organum duplum), while Perotinus' is an organum quadruplum. In Leoninus' organum duplum the upper voice swirls around very freely and melismatically over the drone-like tenor. The incipit alone lasts for a little over four minutes, whereas the entire Gradual takes about nine minutes. In Perotinus' organum quadruplum the chant is again sung in lengthened notes by the bottom voice; the upper three voices move together like chords, and a new element, metrical rhythm, is introduced. Indeed, the rhythm has a jaunty, dance-like character to it, and the modern equivalent would be 6/8 meter; the text is from Psalm 98 (97):3, 2.

Soloists	Choir	Soloists	Choir
Polyph.	Chant	Polyphony	Chant
Vidérunt omnes	Fines terræ salutáre Dei nostri: jubiláte Deo omnis terra.	Notum fecit Dóminus salutáre suum: ante conspéctum géntium revelávit	justítiam suam.

All the ends of the earth have seen the salvation of our God.
Be joyful in God all the whole earth.
The Lord has declared His salvation. His righteousness hath
He openly shewed in the sight of the heathen.

In Perotinus' *Viderunt omnes*, the sonic effect of the very active and regularly rhythmic upper voices over the drone-like chant melody is mesmerizing and somewhat mystical. To carry on with the analogy to architecture, the organum quadruplum (and organum triplum) can be seen to correspond to the new Gothic style in which, in its tendency to go ever higher, the nave became much more elevated and arches were now pointed. Rather than the thick walls and small windows of Romanesque churches, Gothic buildings were able to soar, despite thinner walls, thanks to flying buttresses that supported them, and much larger stained-glass windows. The organum quadruplum could be compared to the four storys of an early Gothic cathedral like Notre-Dame de Paris, which essentially "stacked" arches of various sizes and levels of ornamentation—arcade, tribune, triforium, and clerestory—one on top of another, like the vertical, chordal voices of the organum quadruplum.

To close this chapter, I will briefly mention a master of polyphony and poetry in the late Middles Ages, when French polyphony became ever more complex, especially in its rhythmic aspect. The outstanding French musical and poetic genius of the fourteenth century was Guillaume de Machaut (ca. 1300–1377), an ordained canon who was renowned for both his poetry and music (sacred and secular). Such an eminent poet as Geoffrey Chaucer emulated Guillaume's verse, and the canon's many secular songs—like his lively *Douce dame jolie* (Sweet pretty lady)—were prized at European courts. His grandest composition is his *Messe de Nostre Dame* (Mass of Our Lady), which is considered to be the first setting of the Mass Ordinary known to have been composed as a complete entity by a single composer.[3] Guillaume de Machaut spent the last thirty years of his life in his native region as a canon of Reims cathedral. An eighteenth-century copy of Guillaume's will stipulates that a Requiem Mass be sung for him and his brother Jean (also a canon) every Saturday—in honor of the Blessed Virgin—in a side chapel of the cathedral.

---

3   Historically, manuscripts had kept each Ordinary chant by genre, e.g., all the Kyries, all the Glorias, etc.

6

Saint Joan of Arc and Her Musical Contemporaries: English and Burgundian Music of the Late Middle Ages

The Hundred Years' War, lasting from 1337 to 1453, spanned more than one hundred years but consisted of three phases. The third phase, known as the "Lancastrian War," began in 1415 with the Battle of Agincourt, celebrated in Shakespeare's *Henry V*. In fact, a rousing song celebrating this victory exists in two fifteenth-century manuscripts. The "Agincourt Carol" has a Latin refrain (burden), *Deo gracias Anglia* (Give thanks, England, to God), for three voices, interspersed with two-voice stanzas in Middle English. It was in 1429, during this Lancastrian War, that the teenaged Jeanne d'Arc (ca. 1412–1431) joined and became influential in the French forces. She became a catalyst in turning the tables so that eventually the English were routed and France regained all her territory. The music of England and Burgundy was intertwined, thanks to historical events, and English music had a great impact on the music of continental Europe during the fourteenth and fifteenth centuries for reasons both political and artistic.

Since the Battle of Hastings and the Norman conquest of England, there had been much interchange between the two cultures. Notre Dame polyphony was known to the British, and the English style, conversely, became known on the continent. The temporary defeat of the French in the Battle of Agincourt brought many English lords to the continent with their households. Last, and perhaps more conclusively, the conciliar movement in the Church brought English bishops,

45

their chaplains, and other musicians to continental Europe for the Council of Constance (1414–1418).

French and Burgundian composers noticed something distinctive about English music, which came to be known as the *contenance angloise*. The poet Martin Le Franc (ca. 1410–1461) coined the term in the following excerpt from his poem *Le Champion des Dames*.[1]

Tapissier, Carmen, Cesaris
Na pas longtmeps si bien
chanterrent
Quilz esbahirent tout paris
Et tous ceulx qui les
frequenterrent;
Mais oncques jour ne
deschanterrent
En melodie de tels chois
Ce mont dit qui les hanterrent
Que G. Du Fay et Binchois.
Car ilz ont nouvelle pratique de
faire frisque concordance
En haulte et en basse musique
en
faint, en pause, et en muance
*Et one prins de **la contenance***
***Angloise** et ensuy Dunstable*
Pour quoy merveilleuse
plaisance
Rend leur chant joyeux et
notable.

Tapissier, Carmen, Cesaris
Not long ago so well did sing
That they astonished all Paris
And all who came fore-
gathering.
But still their discant held no
strain
Filled with such goodly
melody—
So folk who heard them now
maintain—
As Binchois sings, or Dufay.
For these a newer way have
found,
In music high and music low,
Of making pleasant concord
sound—
In "feigning," rests, mutatio.
The English guise they wear
with grace,
They follow Dunstable aright,
And thereby have they learnt
apace
To make their music gay and
bright.

---

1   Quoted in Gustave Reese, *Music in the Renaissance*, 2nd ed. (New York: W. W. Norton, 1958), 12–13.

Among the names of composers in the above passage there are three that are worth noting. Two were the most notable Burgundian composers of that day: "G. Du fay" was Guillaume Du Fay (1397–1474), of whom we will learn more later, and Gilles Binchois (ca. 1400–1460). Martin Le Franc notes how these two composers "took on the guise of the English" (*contenance angloise*) and that their leader was John Dunstable (ca. 1385–1453), a composer we shall meet shortly.

During the Hundred Years' War, especially after Henry V's victory at Agincourt (1415), the English spent much time on the continent. During these years, Burgundy was the ally of England against France. Dunstable might have influenced French and Burgundian music during his years as a singer in the chapel of John, Duke of Bedford, who was regent of France from 1423 to 1429 and governor of Normandy from 1429 to 1435. It was Bedford, in fact, who was responsible for the condemnation of Jeanne d'Arc as a heretic. In 1423, the Duke of Bedford strengthened the alliance between England and Burgundy by marrying Anne of Burgundy, the sister of Philip the Good, Duke of Burgundy. So, it is possible that Dunstable could even have met Du Fay and Binchois in Burgundy and had an influence on Burgundian music.

Just what was it that made English music so attractive to the French and Burgundians? Generally, English music was more popular in style. Melodies were simpler, with regular phrasing, and rhythm was not so complex as in French vocal music. The voices tended to move in a fuller, chordal texture, and text settings were mostly syllabic. But it was the harmony that was especially appealing, as English music featured more use of the intervals of a third and a sixth. In fact, passages of parallel thirds and sixths—known as faburden—were tonal-sounding in contrast to the Continental sound, which was modal and featured more fourths and fifths, based on ancient Pythagorean theory.

A beautiful example of the *contenance angloise* is John Dunstable's three-voice motet *Quam pulchra es*. It is a Marian

votive antiphon, a fifth in addition to the standard four antiphons (*Alma Redemptoris mater, Ave Regina cælorum, Regina
cæli*, and *Salve Regina*) that was customarily sung after Com-
pline in late medieval Franciscan and Roman liturgical uses
between the Nativity of the Virgin (September 8) and the
Saturday before the First Sunday of Advent. In other words,
Quam pulchra es took the place of *Salve Regina* during the
last part of the liturgical year. Its lyrics are from the Song of
Songs (7:6, 7, 5, 4, 11, 12), an Old Testament book of love
poems that have symbolic meanings. Relevant here is that the
Church has accommodated these texts for the celebration of
Marian feasts.

The Duchy of Burgundy was one of the major players in
European history of the fifteenth century. The geographical
areas of Burgundy comprised east-central France (their original lands), Holland, Belgium, northeastern France, Lux-
embourg, and Lorraine. The official capital was Dijon, but
after about 1450 the court had several temporary locations,
including Lille, Bruges, Ghent, and Brussels. The dukes of
Burgundy, although vassals of the French kings, were actually
their equals in terms of power. Throughout the fourteenth
and fifteenth centuries, until 1477, when the last duke died
without a successor, Burgundy greatly expanded its territory.
The dukes of Burgundy were enormously wealthy and spent
much money on the arts wherever their court happened to
be situated. Their chapel set the European standard for opu-
lence and musical excellence during the last half of the fifteenth century. In 1384, Duke Philip the Bold established
the chapel, and by 1445, under the reign of Philip the Good,
it had twenty-three singers, which was a large number then.
At that time a chapel was not a specifically religious institution, but the members, mostly all clerics, carried out various tasks for their noble employers. Because the dukes of
Burgundy lived such a peripatetic existence, the cities where

they had their courts became renowned centers for music and musical instruction.

Guillaume Du Fay (ca. 1397–1474), the most illustrious musician in all of fifteenth-century Europe, was associated with the Burgundian court, though probably only through an honorary appointment to the ducal chapel. He was educated at the cathedral school of Cambrai from 1409 to 1412 and returned there in his forties after working most of his life in Italy and Savoy. In the fourteenth century, Cambrai, in the northernmost part of France, was hemmed in by Burgundian territories, and its cathedral was known for the high quality of its music. Finishing his musical education, Du Fay migrated south, where he served in the chapels of the popes and of the dukes of Savoy, between which there were often disputes, and which sometimes put the composer in a delicate position. He composed both sacred and secular music, but this chapter will focus on a work of Du Fay that had both religious and civic significance, his motet *Nuper rosarum flores/Terribilis est locus iste*. The double title reflects the fact that two different texts are used. The civic significance of the motet is that it was composed for the reconsecration of the cathedral of Florence, Italy, on March 25, 1436. Constructed over the site of the previous cathedral (Santa Reparata), the Cathedral of Santa Maria del Fiore was begun in 1296 by Arnolfo di Cambio but was not consecrated until 1436, upon completion of the now famous dome designed by Filippo Brunelleschi (1377–1446).

Guillaume Du Fay's *Nuper rosarum flores* is a four-voice motet for *Triplum* (Soprano), *Motetus* (Alto), *Tenor I*, and *Tenor II*. The motet is a remarkable edifice that mirrors the dimensions of the cathedral, according to several scholars.

The two lower voices sing, in canon, a *cantus firmus* (pre-composed melody), the first phrase of the Gregorian chant *Terribilis est locus iste*, Introit for the Mass for the dedication of a church. The text is a phrase uttered by Jacob in Genesis

28:17, when he paused for a night during his journey to his
uncle Laban's in Haran, where he was to find a wife. During
this dream, wherein Jacob sees angels ascending and descending a ladder, God tells him that the land on which he is sleeping will become his, that his descendants shall multiply, and
that all nations shall be blessed by Jacob and his descendants.

Terribilis est locus iste!	How awesome is this shrine!
Hic domus Dei est,	It is the house of God,
et porta cæli.	and the gateway to heaven.

The two upper voices sing melodies composed by Du Fay, set
to four poetic stanzas of seven lines each, possibly written by
the composer himself. They describe the dedicatory event and
its circumstances.

Nuper rosarum flores	Recently roses [came]
Ex dono pontificis	As a gift of the Pope,
Hieme licet horrida,	Although in cruel winter,
Tibi, virgo coelica,	To you, heavenly Virgin.
Pie et sancte deditum	Dutifully and blessedly is
Grandis templum machinæ	dedicated
Condecorarunt perpetim.	[to you] a temple of magnificent
	design.
	May they together be perpetual
	ornaments.

Hodie vicarius	Today the Vicar
Jesu Christi et Petri	Of Jesus Christ and Peter's
Successor EUGENIUS	Successor, EUGENIUS,
Hoc idem amplissimum	This same most spacious
Sacris templum manibus	Sacred temple with his hands
Sanctisque liquorib us	And with holy waters
Consecrare dignatus est.	He is worthy to consecrate.

Igitur, alma parens,	Therefore, gracious parent,
Nati tui et filia,	And daughter of your offspring,
Virgo decus virginum,	Virgin, ornament of virgins,
Tuus te FLORENTIÆ	your, Florence's, people
Devotus orat populus,	Devoutly pray
Ut qui mente et corpore	So that together with all mankind,
Mundo quicquam exoravit.	With mind and body,
	Their entreaties may move you.
Oratione tua	Through your prayer,
Cruciatus et meritis	your anguish and merits,
Tui secundum carnem	may [we] deserve
Nati Domini sui	to receive of the Lord,
Grata beneficia	Born of you according to the flesh,
Veniamque reatum	the benefits of grace
Accipere mereatur.	and the remission of sins.
Amen.	Amen.

The first stanza refers to the golden roses that popes have occasionally conferred on designated churches or individuals. This gift is traditionally given on Lætare Sunday, the Fourth Sunday of Lent, the Sunday on which rose-colored vestments are worn. Pope Eugenius IV had presented the rose just one week earlier, probably Lætare Sunday that year. But March 25 was also the Annunciation and, in the local calendar, New Year's Day. Stanza 2 mentions the reconsecration, with holy water, of the Duomo, and the last two stanzas are petitions to the Blessed Virgin. It's hard to imagine a more splendid liturgical occasion, with the dignified and beautiful polyphony of Du Fay sung in a cathedral of peerless artistic beauty ushering in the Glory of God. Even the procession must have been glorious, with Pope Eugenius and his court, along with local churchmen, including the Dominicans, among whom might have been Saint Antoninus and Blessed Giovanni of Fiesole (aka Fra Angelico). It's no wonder that later, in 1467, Piero de' Medici would describe Du Fay as "the greatest ornament of our age,"[2] which is quite a tribute when one realizes that this was also the age of artists such as Botticelli, Donatello, and Fra Angelico.

---

2   Quoted in David Fallows, *Dufay* (New York: Vintage Books, 1988), 1.

7

A Renaissance Beethoven?
Josquin Des Prez and the
Franco-Flemish Sound

Francesco Petrarca (1304–1379) is commonly acknowledged as the father of humanism and idea of rebirth—seen as the restorer of classical studies. Petrarch discarded the medieval Catholic notion that saw history in terms of a succession of the light of Christ over ancient pagan darkness. After his discovery of a collection of Cicero's letters, Petrarch looked to classical antiquity as a period of light in comparison with the preceding and present eras, for which he coined the term "Dark Ages." Petrarch presented the concept of "rebirth," or "Renaissance" (*rinascimento*), an attractive model to other scholars and to artists. Thus, a new era dawned as humanists pored over and translated Greek and Roman manuscripts and artists modeled their paintings and sculptures on classical models. Thanks to these humanists, classical Latin became the ideal, and medieval Latin was denigrated.

Painters, architects, and sculptors had surviving classical sculptures, vase paintings, and architecture to imitate in their desires to emulate classical models. But what about musicians and composers? Only a few fragments of ancient Greek music existed, and these were in notations that needed to be deciphered. The only ancient musical sources available to fifteenth-century musicians were philosophical writings by Plato and Aristotle, or theoretical treatises by the likes of Cleonides, Aristoxenus, and Ptolemy of Alexandria. For Christians, Gregorian chant could be analogized to classical antiquity, just as the patristic writers could be revered along with classical writers. However, by the 1400s the repertory of Gregorian chant was more or less complete and composers were focusing their energy and creativity on mensural polyphony, that is, the most up-to-date version, which featured a regular, straightforward system of meter. There was no music like this in ancient Greece or Rome—nor in the early Church. Musicians, therefore, decided to turn to predecessors from more recent eras for models of "rebirth" to emulate.

Johannes Tinctoris (ca. 1435–1511), a Flemish composer and music theorist, illustrated this tendency in his 1477 book *Liber de arte contrapuncti* (*Book of the Art of Counterpoint*), when he wrote that

> it is a matter of great surprise that there is no composition written over forty years ago which is thought by the learned to be worthy of performance. At this very time ... an infinite number of composers such as Johannes Ockeghem [d. 1497], Johannes Régis [d. 1485], Antoine Busnois [d. 1492], Firmin [or Philippe] Caron [d. 1475], and Guillaume Faugues [d. 1475], who glory in having had as teachers in this divine art the recently departed John Dunstable, Gilles Binchois, and Guillaume Dufay. Almost all the works of those men exhale such sweetness that, in my opinion, they should be considered most worthy, not only of men and heroes, but even of the immortal gods. Certainly, I never listen to them or study them without coming away refreshed and wiser. Just as Virgil took Homer as his model in his divine *Aeneid*, so, by Hercules, do I use these as models for my own small productions; I have, in particular, openly imitated their admirable style of composition with regard to the placement of consonances.[1]

---

1   Johannes Tinctoris, *Liber de arte contrapuncti* [1477], trans. Albert Seay (Rome: American Institute of Musicology, 1961), 14–15, quoted in Piero Weiss and Richard Taruskin, *Music in the Western World: A History in Documents*, 2nd ed. (Belmont, CA: Schirmer Cengage Learning, 2008), 68.

The composers whom Tinctoris admires and cites are all of the generation just prior to Josquin Des Prez (ca. 1450–1521), and their English and Burgundian teachers are from an even earlier generation. Notice how Tinctoris reveals his humanistic orientation by interlarding his remarks with references to ancient writers, and even to "the immortal gods." Notice, too, how he rhapsodizes about the "sweetness" of their music. This was a new element that recognized the "right" for the ear to enjoy music simply for its aural beauty and not just for its intellectual and mystical Pythagorean construction. Medieval composers prescribed the "perfection" of Pythagorean intervals, the second, fourth, and fifth, which they understood as consonant, while they understood the third and the sixth as dissonant. This changeover to aural delight in musical sound can be compared to the portrayal of nature and human anatomy in Renaissance painting. The paintings of Leonardo da Vinci (1452–1519)—an almost exact contemporary of Josquin Des Prez (1450–1521)—exhibit naturalism, compared to the two-dimensional, icon-like appearance of medieval/Romanesque painting.

A new and illustrious generation of composers—known as the Franco-Flemish (or Netherlands) composers, products of the music educational system established by the dukes of Burgundy during their territorial expansion—would become the most sought-after musicians on the European continent. Every court—secular or sacred—wanted to employ these composers: Josquin Des Prez, Jacob Obrecht, Heinrich Isaac, and others.

Josquin Des Prez is probably the most illustrious of them, and in his music this sweetness is fully realized. A celebrated example is Josquin's four-voice motet, *Ave Maria ... Virgo serena*, which was popular even during the composer's lifetime. For example, in 1502 the printer Ottaviano Petrucci placed it at the beginning of a collection of Josquin's motets—the very first printed in movable type. *Ave Maria ... Virgo serena* survives in more than two dozen manuscripts throughout western and central Europe.

The motet is divided into three sections: a five-stanza poem framed by two shorter segments of two lines each. The first two lines quote the words and paraphrase the melody of *Ave Maria … Virgo serena*, the Gregorian chant sequence for the Feast of the Annunciation. The poem in the middle section, *Ave cuius conceptio*, is a rhymed and metered Marian votive antiphon of five stanzas that expands upon the greeting of the archangel Gabriel to our Lady, as each stanza begins with "Ave." Moreover, each quatrain has the same structure: the first three lines include an attribute, or an event, in the life of our Lady, along with the name of the feast related to this. Stanzas 2–5 each end with an application of the event or feast day to our own lives. This poem can be found in a number of Books of Hours, abbreviated versions of the Divine Office for laity (today's *Magnificat* could be considered a modern equivalent). After the poem, the final two lines are an intercessory petition to the Virgin.

Ave Maria, Gratia plena, *Dominus tecum, Virgo serena.*	Hail Mary, full of grace, The Lord is with thee, serene Virgin.
Ave, cuius CONCEPTIO, *Solemni plena gaudio,* *Caelestia, Terrestria,* *Nova replet laetitia.*	Hail, thou whose CONCEPTION, Full of great joy, Fills heaven and earth With new gladness.
Ave, cuius NATIVITAS *Nostra fuit solemnitas,* *Ut lucifer lux oriens* *Verum solem praeveniens.*	Hail, thou whose NATIVITY Became our great celebration, As the light-bearing Morning Star anticipates the true Sun.

Ave pia humilitas,	Hail, faithful humility,
Sine viro fecunditas,	Fruitful without man,
Cuius ANNUNTIATIO	Whose ANNUNCIATION
Nostra fuit salvatio.	Was our salvation.
Ave vera virginitas,	Hail, true virginity,
Immaculata castitas,	Immaculate chastity,
Cuius PURIFICATIO	Whose PURIFICATION
Nostra fuit purgatio.	Was our cleansing.
Ave, praeclara omnibus	Hail, glorious one
Angelicis virtutibus,	In all angelic virtues,
Cuius fuit ASSUMPTIO	Whose ASSUMPTION
Nostra fuit glorificatio.	Was our glorification.
O Mater Dei,	O Mother of God,
Memento mei. Amen.	Remember me. Amen.

In each of the seven sections of his motet, Josquin uses a different musical treatment, which differentiates and articulates the text. As mentioned, the first two lines quote the text and paraphrase—that is, quote the melody but with embellishments—the sequence chant for the Feast of the Annunciation. The four voices are set in imitation—that is, one voice sings the melody and then each other voice follows, imitating the melody of the first voice. In this case, it's the soprano who enters first, followed by the alto, then tenor, and finally bass. This imitative section furnishes a fitting *exordium*, or introduction, to Josquin's motet. Following this, each of the sections of the poem starts with *Ave*, always keeping us in mind of Gabriel's salutation to the Blessed Virgin. Imitation is a cornerstone of Renaissance polyphony, and Josquin was one of its first masters.

 Ave cuius conceptio begins with a duet for soprano and alto; the alto begins with the same notes as the second phrase of the chant sequence. This duet is imitated by tenor and bass, but to add variety Josquin has the alto sing a short melody against them. Rejoicing in the Immaculate Conception, all four voices then sing together in chordal style (homophony) at the words "Solemni plena gaudio." At "cælestia terrestria," the voices break out once again in imitation and begin their ascent in pitch, which reaches the highest pitch in the next phrase, "nova replet lætitia." At *Ave cuius nativitas* Josquin follows the same pattern he used in *Ave cuius conceptio*, where he begins with duet texture (paired imitation) but then—at "ut lucifer lux oriens"—expands into four-voice imitative texture. This time, however, the four voices follow a descending pattern, symbolizing either the humility of the light-bearing Morning Star (Mary), or the humility of the true Sun (Jesus). Each phrase of the fourth stanza (*Ave pia humilitas, Cuius annuntiatio*) descends, which beautifully symbolizes the humility of our Lady at the Annunciation. This stanza is completely in duet format and each phrase is sung only once, thereby shortening this stanza, which now leads into something completely different. *Ave vera virginitas* is set completely in chordal style, and in triple meter, except that the tenor always sings his line just one beat behind the other voices as he is singing a canon with the soprano. The "unanimity" of the chordal style may suggest the *Purificatio* of the Virgin, and the triple meter may symbolize the Trinity. Finally we reach the fifth stanza, which celebrates the highest honor to our Lady—her Assumption. Here Josquin returns to the paired imitation of voices singing duets, until the final line, "Nostra fuit glorificatio," when Josquin uses a full, four-voice texture. After this line, which tells of our glorification through Mary's Assumption, Josquin sets the final two short lines of text, an intercession to the Blessed Virgin: "O Mother of God, remember me." Our own humility before God and His mother is represented in a chordal texture of the three lower voices singing longer, and thus slower, note values. Josquin achieves much musical variety in his motet through the contrast of sections that are imitative with sections that are chordal (homophonic); yet it is done in a way that is smooth and natural, a hallmark of his greatness and his influence on succeeding generations of composers.

But what of my comparison of Josquin to Beethoven? Our conventional impression of Beethoven is that of a composer whose musical style is at the cusp of two eras and who is said to have had a temperamental, dramatic, and stormy personality. The account below—from September 2, 1502—is by one Gian de Artiganova, an agent of the Duke of Ferrara (Ercole I d'Este) who was sent out to find a new musician for the duke's court.

> We have promised him [Heinrich Isaac, another brilliant Franco-Flemish composer] ten ducats a month, and he is satisfied with that; so would you now be so kind as to send word as to whether you are in agreement with all this or not. He seemed to me far more suitable to serve Your Highness than Josquin, since he is more sociable with his colleagues and composes new things more quickly. It is true that Josquin is the better composer, but he writes only when he pleases, not when he is requested to, and has demanded 200 ducats in salary, while Isaac is content with 120. Your Highness can now choose between them at pleasure.[2]

The duke decided to hire Josquin, who composed some of his greatest music while in Ferrara. Josquin left in 1504 after an outbreak of the plague and returned to his native French territory of Condé-sur-l'Escaut, close to modern-day Belgium.

---

2   Helmuth Osthoff, *Josquin des Prez* (Tutzing: H. Schneider, 1962), I, 211–12, trans. Richard Taruskin and quoted in Piero Weiss and Richard Taruskin, *Music in the Western World: A History in Documents*, 2nd ed. (Belmont, CA: Schirmer Cengage Learning, 2008), 84.

Josquin's replacement was Jacob Obrecht, another great Franco-Flemish composer who died from plague in 1505. Josquin spent the rest of his days as provost of the church of Notre-Dame, which was destroyed in 1793, along with Josquin's grave.

8

Music in Counter-Reformation Rome

The Council of Trent (1545–1563) was a defining moment for the Catholic Church. Music—along with other arts—was employed to win back Catholics seduced by Protestantism. Concerning liturgical music, the Council Fathers made no explicit rules; discussion of music was left until the council's final sessions. Practically, the only stricture of the council was against secular elements in liturgical music, and implementation of the official Canons was left to diocesan authorities. The question of intelligibility of liturgical texts was vigorously discussed by the Council Fathers but never appeared in the council's official Canons. Understanding the words was important both to Christian humanists and to leaders of the Counter-Reformation in reevangelizing Europe. Music was seen as a vehicle of evangelization, so long as music remained the servant of the words.

The leading composers of liturgical music in Counter-Reformation Rome were Giovanni Pierluigi da Palestrina, the Spaniard Tomás Luis de Victoria, and three sets of brothers—Giovanni and Paolo Animuccia, Giovanni Maria and Giovanni Bernardino Nanino, and Felice and Giovanni Francesco Anerio. Palestrina (ca. 1525–1594) came of age as the Council of Trent was beginning, and most of his works consist of sacred music, either for liturgical or devotional use. Many of the extra-liturgical devotional activities of confraternities inspired Palestrina to compose polychoral works—music for multiple choirs set to psalms, litanies, and Marian antiphons. In addition, forty-nine of his 140-plus madrigals are spiritual madrigals with sacred Italian lyrics, intended for personal spiritual recreational or devotional use.

The early 1600s saw the establishment of Palestrina's reputation as the ideal composer of *a cappella* (i.e., unaccompanied) polyphony, designated *stile antico*. The emergence around 1600 of a new style (*stile nuovo*) of sacred music indebted to secular music styles—particularly opera—brought about a renewed focus on Palestrina's imitative polyphonic style as a thing of the past, and yet something to be revered and imitated. If a composer were to use this learned style in his sacred music, or even within secular music, he could win approval for retaining a style of polyphonic music that was perceived to be more sacred.

Palestrina's entire life was spent in or near Rome. Because of his surname it is thought that he was born in Palestrina, an ancient town approximately twenty-two miles east of Rome. His earliest musical training was as a choirboy at the church of Santa Maria Maggiore—one of the four major basilicas of Rome. Palestrina began his professional career in October 1544 as organist for the Cathedral of San Agapito in Palestrina. In 1547, while still at the cathedral, Palestrina married Lucrezia Gori, a local girl. By 1551, when Palestrina left this position, he and Lucrezia had two sons, Rodolfo and Angelo. A third son, Iginio, was born in 1558 and was the only one to outlive his father.

On September 1, 1551, Pope Julius III, formerly bishop of Palestrina, appointed the composer *magister cantorum* of the Cappella Giulia. Palestrina was not required to produce compositions for this job, although in 1552 he published his first book of Masses, which was dedicated to the pope. Evidently, Julius was so pleased that he had Palestrina added to the *Cappella Sistina* in January 1555. But the pope breached the rules

by appointing Palestrina in that he was a married man, in that
he had not been examined, and in that the other choristers
had not consented. Julius died on March 23, and his successor, Marcellus II, died after a pontificate of only twenty-two
days, so by September Palestrina, along with two other married singers, had been dismissed by Pope Paul IV. Palestrina
did not have long to wait before he was hired again, this time
as *maestro* of the Lateran Basilica, Rome's cathedral; this job
lasted till July 1560. Returning to Santa Maria Maggiore, Palestrina worked there until around 1565.

Finally, in 1571 Palestrina was back at the Cappella Giulia,
where he stayed until his death. In the 1570s tragedy struck
Palestrina when the plague took his sons Rodolfo and Angelo,
and in 1580 his wife. At this point Palestrina considered the
priesthood, but his vocation plans changed, however, when in
1581 Palestrina married a wealthy widow, Virginia Dormoli.
Now he was liberated from financial concerns associated with
the salary of a choirmaster.

Palestrina's vast output for the Church includes 104 *many works*
Masses, three hundred-plus motets, sixty-eight settings of
Offertory antiphons, about seventy-two hymns, thirty-five
Magnificats, eleven litanies, and several sets of Lamentations
for *Tenebræ* in Holy Week. In his sacred music Palestrina
sought to serve the liturgy and embody the musical ideals of
the Counter-Reformation by making the words intelligible
through many passages in homophonic (chordal) texture and
by contrasting different groupings of voices. But this cannot
describe the richness and variety of Palestrina's style. The
purity and balance of his musical style can be seen in melodic
lines of predominantly stepwise motion, resulting in a smooth
sound. If the composer uses a skip or a leap, it is usually followed by a step or skip in the opposite direction. Palestrina's
masterful use of counterpoint and control of dissonance in
works like his motet *Super flumina Babylonis* earned him the

nickname *princeps musicæ*. His control of dissonance ensures that there will be no unprepared, harsh dissonances, but it is so carefully managed and so subtle as never to be boring. Palestrina's music, in a Platonic way, mirrors divine perfection through its own perfection of form and serves the liturgy by never drawing attention to itself. Pope Saint John Paul II said of Palestrina: "It would seem that, after a troubled period, the Church regained a voice made peaceful through contemplation of the Eucharistic mystery, like the calm breathing of a soul that knows it is loved by God."[1]

In 1537, when the teenaged Philip (Filippo) Neri left his native Florence for Rome, he took with him the Florentine traditions of popular piety in which he had been reared. His father, Francesco, had been a follower of the Dominican friar Girolamo Savonarola, whose memory still remained strong in Florence. Francesco sent Philip to the Dominican convent of San Marco where, surrounded by the frescoes of Fra Angelico, Filippo received his secondary education. One of his friar-teachers, Servatio Mini, was an author of *laude spirituali*—popular religious songs in Italian or Latin—and it is certain that Filippo learned to sing *laude* at home and school.

Many Romans were active in confraternities, including Palestrina, who in 1548 joined the lay archconfraternity of *Santissima Trinità dei Pellegrini*. It had been recently begun by Philip Neri, who commissioned them to start an apostolate to pilgrims. So many pilgrims were helped that the confraternity eventually built the church of *Santa Trinità dei Pellegrini* from 1587 to 1616.[2]

Upon his priestly ordination in 1551, Filippo moved to the church of San Girolamo della Carità and here he began to hold prayer and discussion meetings for young men. Their

1   Address of His Holiness John Paul II to the Plenary Assembly of the Pontifical Council for Culture (March 18, 1994), no. 8.

2   In 2008 Benedict XVI assigned it to the care of the Priestly Fraternity of Saint Peter.

meeting room was called the Oratory (*Oratorio*, from *orare*, "to pray"), and thus began in 1556 what eventually became the Congregation of the Oratory.

The year 1575 was a watershed year in Counter-Reformation Rome; it was the year in which Saint Philip Neri founded the Congregation of the Oratory, his community of secular priests, and its statutes were approved by Pope Gregory XVIII. The devotional life of Roman citizens flourished, thanks mainly to the Oratory. Palestrina is not known to have composed any *laude*, but he was a friend of Neri and is known to have participated in music at the Oratory. Philip knew music's value in the formation of souls, and the singing of *laude* became a regular feature of Oratorian spiritual exercises. These varied in accord with the liturgical season or the time of day, but the three primary components were readings, a sermon, and *laude*.

Giovanni Animuccia (ca. 1500–1571), a Florentine, had lived in Rome since about midcentury. He was chapelmaster at the Cappella Giulia between Palestrina's two periods of employment there, and his liturgical music is considered to be comparable with Palestrina's. Animuccia and his wife became lay followers of Neri; in 1570 he became chapelmaster of the Oratory. His two publications of *laude* illustrate the popularity of the Oratory movement and the benefits of having a professional musician at the Oratory. His first book of *laude* (1563) featured simple four-voice works in chordal texture, designed, as Animuccia wrote in his preface, "for the consolation and needs of many spiritual and devout persons, religious and secular."[3] The second volume, issued in 1570, had more musically sophisticated contents, which Animuccia explained was because the Oratory had grown "with the

---

3   Quoted in Lewis Lockwood, "Animuccia, Giovanni," *The New Grove Dictionary of Music and Musicians*, vol. I, ed. Stanley Sadie (London: Macmillan, 1995), 437.

coming together of prelates and the most important gentle-men."[4] Other musicians active at the Oratory were Maurizio Anerio and his sons Felice (ca. 1560–1614) and Giovanni Francesco (ca. 1567–1630), both of whom would later become significant composers. Giovanni Francesco contrib-uted to the next stage of musical development at the Oratory, especially through his publication *Teatro armonico spirituale* (1619), in which the later musical genre of the oratorio can be seen in its earliest form, as a dramatic dialogue on the par-able of the prodigal son.

Sometime between 1563 and 1565, the young Spaniard Tomás Luis de Victoria (ca. 1548–1611) left his hometown of Àvila for Rome, to study at the Collegium Germanicum. This institution trained young Germans as missionaries to stem the spread of Lutheranism, but it also housed seminar-ians from Italy, Spain, and England. At this time Palestrina was chapelmaster of the nearby Roman Seminary; thus, one can assume that Victoria not only knew Palestrina but also studied with him. From 1569 Victoria served as singer and organist at several Roman churches and chapels until 1573, when the Germanicum appointed him *maestro di cappella* and music teacher to the German seminarians; the young Spaniard would have taught them in Latin.

In 1575 Victoria was ordained a priest by Bishop Thomas Goldwell, the last remaining bishop from pre-Reformation England. Following ordination Victoria joined the Congrega-tion of the Oratory, where he was a resident priest from 1578 to 1585. Though Victoria composed exclusively sacred music, he is not known to have composed any *laude* for the Oratory.

Those years saw many publications of Victoria's music—Masses, motets, hymns, Magnificats, and the Office for Holy Week. His Mass settings were in demand all over Europe, and

---

4   Ibid.

even the Protestant Englishman Henry Peacham remarked that "for composition I prefer next [after William Byrd] Ludovico de Victoria, a most judicious and a sweet composer."[5] New World choirmasters also sought Victoria's music. In Mexico City his music was sung so often that the choir's partbooks wore out and had to be replaced.

Victoria's music has been likened in its mystical fervor to the paintings of El Greco, a near contemporary of the composer. Some of Victoria's motets contain plangent, dramatic flourishes of word painting, a technique borrowed from madrigal composers. Motets like *O vos omnes*, with lyrics from the Lamentations of Jeremiah, have given Victoria a reputation for seriousness and mysticism; his contemporaries, though, saw him in a different light. King John IV of Portugal noted that "although there is much in his Holy Week volume that exactly suits the text, nonetheless his disposition being naturally sunny he never stays downcast for long."[6] Many of Victoria's works, for example, *Hosanna filio David* and *O quam gloriosum*, shine with Christian joy. Perhaps it was his contact with Saint Philip Neri that affected Victoria's disposition, but perhaps— conversely—it was his own sunny disposition that drew him toward the lighthearted saint of Rome and the Oratory.

What a time to have been in Rome when the Church was full of reforming zeal and saints like Philip Neri. Not only that, but the Eternal City was experiencing a golden period of sacred music.

---

5   Henry Peacham, *The Compleat Gentleman*, quoted in Oliver Strunk, ed., *Source Readings in Music History* (New York: W. W. Norton, 1950), 335.

6   John IV, *Defensa de la música moderna* (1649), trans. and quoted in Robert Stevenson, "Victoria, Tomás Luis de," *The New Grove Dictionary of Music and Musicians*, vol. 19, ed. Stanley Sadie (London: Macmillan, 1995), 709.

9

Catholic Composers and the
Reformation in England

Over three hundred English men and women—religious and
lay—gave their lives for the Catholic faith during the Tudor
and Stuart eras, and out of those, forty were canonized by Pope
Saint Paul VI in 1970 as representatives for the whole glorious company of martyrs. Since the 1534 Act of Supremacy,
when Henry VIII declared himself the head of the Church in
England, many English Catholics, living lives of great danger
and deprivation, continued to adhere to "the old religion."
These recusants, as they came to be called under Elizabeth I,
refused to obey the Uniformity Act of 1558 (passed in 1559),
which required all citizens to attend Anglican services weekly.
During the history of music in England's "golden age," details
of the music and musical life of faithful Catholics are not
plentiful, but readers may find interesting these few vignettes
of secrecy, exile, and imprisonment.

> For motets and music of piety and devotion, as well for the
> honor of our nation as the merit of the man, I prefer above
> all others our phoenix, Mr. William Byrd, whom in that
> kind I know not whether any may equal, I am sure none
> excel, even by the judgment of France and Italy, who are
> very sparing in the commendation of strangers in regard of
> that conceit they hold of themselves. His *Cantiones sacræ*, as
> also his *Gradualia*, are mere angelical and divine, and being
> of himself naturally disposed to gravity and piety his vein is

not so much for light madrigals or canzonets, yet his "Virgi-
nelle" and some others in his First Set cannot be mended by
the best Italian of them all.[1]

Henry Peacham—in his *The Compleat Gentleman*, published
in 1622, the year before William Byrd's death—offers a
glimpse of the composer and of how he was esteemed by his
contemporaries, and hints at his versatility. Peacham, although
a Puritan, rightly focuses on Byrd's sacred music, and while
the composer did not contribute much to the lighter genres
of madrigal and lute song, nevertheless, Byrd's few madrigals,
for example, *Though Amaryllis Dance in Green*, are among the
best in England's madrigalian garden.

Byrd was a Londoner born and bred. It seems likely that he
joined the Chapel Royal as a chorister around 1550; there
he would have been taught composition and keyboard by
the great Thomas Tallis (1505–1585). On March 25, 1562,
Byrd assumed his first position, as organist and choirmaster at
Lincoln Cathedral, and it was here that he married, in 1568.
Within the next decade the Byrds had three sons and a daughter. In 1572 Byrd was sworn in as a Gentleman of the Chapel
Royal; here the composer served as an organist and singing
man at the Anglican services held for Queen Elizabeth I. Both
Byrd and Tallis were Catholic musicians working in a Protestant world. Tallis famously worked "under fower sovraynes,"
and while he composed complex Latin polyphony, he also
wrote simple syllabic masterpieces like *If Ye Love Me*. There is
evidence that Byrd, beginning in 1573, began to count Catholic noblemen, such as Lord Thomas Paget, among his friends.

In 1575 the queen granted a twenty-one-year monopoly
for printing music to Byrd and Tallis, and it was in this year

---

1   Henry Peacham, *The Compleat Gentleman*, quoted in Oliver Strunk, ed., *Source Readings in Music History* (New York: W. W. Norton, 1950), 335.

that they brought out the first volume of *Cantiones, quae ab argumento sacræ vocantur*, a collection of Latin motets by both composers, possibly intended for domestic, devotional use. The capture and execution in 1581 of Saint Edmund Campion, S.J., occasioned much outrage in the Catholic community, and one response was Henry Walpole's poem, "Why Do I Use My Paper, Ink, and Pen?" Byrd's setting of this text was published in his 1588 *Psalms, Sonnets, and Songs of Sadness and Piety*, a collection of English secular and sacred songs for domestic use. William Byrd and the future Saint Edmund Campion were exact contemporaries, Campion having been born in 1540.

William Byrd was relatively protected from the Elizabethan persecution because of the favor he enjoyed as a Gentleman of the Chapel Royal. He was an organist for Queen Elizabeth, and during that time he had composed choral masterpieces with English texts for use in Anglican liturgies. His English anthems like *Sing Joyfully* and *Turn Our Captivity* show the same mastery as his Latin motets, but living a double life must have become onerous for him. Tallis and Byrd issued two volumes of *Cantiones sacrae* in 1589 and 1591, and a number of the motets have texts that contain veiled allusions to the worsening situation of English Catholics. Volume II contains *Exsurge, quare obdormis, Domine*, for example, which uses verses from Psalm 44 (43):23–24 to refer to Catholics' plight.

Exsurge, quare obdormis, Domine?	Arise, O Lord: why sleepest Thou?
Exsurge, et ne repellas me in finem.	Arise, and reject me not for ever.
Quare faciem tuam avertis?	Wherefore hidest Thou Thy face and
Oblivisceris inopiae nostrae et tribulationis nostrae?	Forgettest our misery and
Exsurge, Domine.	trouble? Arise, O Lord!

Byrd began to spend less time in London, but it wasn't until his retirement in 1590 that he assumed a fully Catholic persona. In 1592 he began to compose music for his beleaguered fellow Catholics, beginning with his three settings of the Mass Ordinary. The most ambitious part of his project, though, was an ingeniously devised cycle of liturgical motets—settings of the Mass Propers—for the principal feasts of the Church year—found in his two volumes of *Gradualia*, published in 1605 and 1607. By selecting and rearranging the various musical components, Catholics could have music fitting for their clandestine Masses. In 1594 Byrd moved from his house at Harlington to another at Stondon Massey, Essex, where he joined a Catholic community centered around Ingatestone, the country manor of Sir John Petre. Byrd's powerful connections from his Chapel Royal days kept him from any serious punishment, though he and his family were fined for recusancy.

One of the three hundred English martyrs—though not among the forty canonized—was Henry Garnet, S.J. (1555–1606), who was implicated unfairly in the Gunpowder Plot. Garnet recalled one of the clandestine liturgical celebrations at which music of William Byrd could have been sung, possibly one of his three settings of the Mass and the choral Propers, as published in *Gradualia*. "We kept Corpus Christi day with great solemnity and music, and this day of the Octave made a solemn procession about a great garden."[2] The house (Fremland, manor of Sir John Tyrrel) was watched, but this "we knew not till the next day when we departed."[3] That Byrd and Garnet did know each other is attested by an eyewitness account of the Frenchman Charles de Ligny, who was taken by a Jesuit to a house outside London. There, he

---

2   Quoted in Philip Caraman, *Henry Garnet (1555–1606) and the Gunpowder Plot* (New York: Farrar, Straus & Co., 1964), 320.
3   Ibid.

found Garnet in company with several Jesuits and gentlemen, who were playing music: among them Mr William Byrd, who played the organ and many other instruments. To that house came, chiefly on the solemn days observed by the Papists, many of the nobility and many ladies by coach or otherwise.[4]

One of the most famous manuscripts traditionally associated with recusant Catholics is the Fitzwilliam Virginal Book, a manuscript of almost three hundred secular and sacred works for a type of harpsichord called the virginal, or virginals. All of the contemporary keyboard genres are present, for example, arrangements of songs or madrigals, preludes, fantasias, variations, chant-based works, and many dance forms— pavans, galliards, almans, corantos, and others. The same handwriting is used throughout, and traditionally the author has been thought to be Francis Tregian the Younger (1574– 1619), scion of a distinguished Catholic family from Cornwall. Like many other Catholics, Tregian was educated at the English exile colleges of Eu and Douai. From 1592 to 1594 he served in Rome as chamberlain to William Cardinal Allen. Returning to England, he attempted to reclaim the Cornish lands confiscated from his father, who was exiled in Lisbon, but young Tregian was imprisoned on charges of recusancy. Here Tregian is thought to have compiled the manuscript of keyboard music, and here he stayed until his death in 1619. Among the composers whose works appear in the Fitzwilliam Virginal Book are some who are Catholic or who have Catholic connections—Byrd, Tallis, Dowland, John Bull, and Peter Philips.

Peter Philips (ca. 1560–ca. 1633) was a Catholic composer in exile. After time as a chorister at Saint Paul's

---

4   *Hat. Cal.,* 17, 611 (Calendar of Manuscripts of the Marquess of Salisbury preserved at Hatfield House), quoted in Caraman, *Henry Garnet,* 317.

Cathedral, he left England in 1582, never to return. Upon arriving in Rome, Philips went to the English College, where he worked as organist for the next three years. During this time Philips had much exposure to the music of Palestrina and of Felice Anerio, who became *maestro di cappella* at the English College in 1585. This Roman influence would be evident in Philips' vocal music for the rest of his life. That same year Philips entered the service of Lord Thomas Paget, who had become exiled, and for the next five years, he and Paget lived a peripatetic existence in Genoa, Madrid, France, Antwerp, and Brussels. Finally, in 1589, they settled in Brussels, where Paget died the very next year. Philips then married and moved to Antwerp. He began to make a living as music teacher and composer, but during this time he was accused of being a conspirator in an assassination plot against Queen Elizabeth and he was imprisoned at the Hague. After inquiries in London, Philips was proclaimed innocent and was released.

In the next several years madrigals by Philips were published, and in 1597 he entered the service of Archduke Albert of Austria. Albert and his wife, Isabella of Spain, were joint regents of the southern Netherlands. Their reign was marked by peace and stability, and by a strengthening of Catholic culture. Their court, in addition to Peter Philips, boasted the presence of the painter Peter Paul Rubens. The remaining years of Philips' life saw many publications of his sacred vocal works; in fact, William Byrd was the only English composer more published than Philips during that era. In *The Compleat Gentleman* Henry Peacham paid him tribute.

> Nor must I here forget our rare countryman, Peter Philips, organist to their *altezzas* at Brussels and now one of the greatest masters of music in Europe. He hath sent us over many

excellent songs, as well motets as madrigals. He affecteth altogether the Italian vein.[5]

Philips' keyboard music, however, is mostly from before his exile, and reflects English style. Furthermore, this music was never published and is almost exclusively in the Fitzwilliam Virginal Book.

Around 1617 another English Catholic musician found refuge in Brussels, and perhaps he became acquainted there with Peter Philips.[6] This was Richard Dering (ca. 1580–1630), who became organist to the English Benedictine nuns in Brussels. Unlike Philips, however, Dering did return to England when he was hired as organist to the Catholic Queen Henrietta Maria, wife of Charles I, in 1625. It is also recorded that Dering functioned as a "musician for the lutes and voices"[7] to the king. His only published music was in the Italian style, and his Latin motets for two and three voices were so popular that in 1662, thirty-two years after Dering's death, the publisher John Playford published *Cantica sacra*, a set of some motets that had been circulating in manuscript for years.

There are many riches to discover in the works of these two expatriate Catholic composers and in the Fitzwilliam Virginal Book, a fruit of imprisonment for the Catholic faith. The music of Byrd and Tallis is also an inspiring testament to two composers who stayed in England and were never imprisoned, but who bravely worked under parlous conditions.

5   Henry Peacham, *The Compleat Gentleman*, quoted in Oliver Strunk, ed., *Source Readings in Music History* (New York: W. W. Norton, 1950), 336.

6   Also present was John Bull, another keyboard virtuoso who had fled to the Low Countries to escape charges of adultery, but who claimed he was fleeing because of his Catholicism.

7   Peter Platt, "Dering, Richard," *The New Grove Dictionary of Music and Musicians*, vol. 5, ed. Stanley Sadie (London: Macmillan, 1995), 382.

10

Monteverdi:
A Composer astride Two Centuries

Philosophical discussions and musical experimentation among Italian humanists dominated the last decade of the sixteenth century, especially in Florence. This decade could be thought of as the cusp of the Baroque era in music as humanists like Vincenzo Galilei (father of Galileo Galilei) argued against the thick texture of both sacred and secular polyphony, which made the words unintelligible to listeners. These humanists, of course, looked back to ancient Greece for inspiration, and Vincenzo argued that the most intelligible and most properly dramatic vocal music would be a single vocal line with a chordal accompaniment. Galilei was a member of the Florentine Camerata, a group of men of letters who regularly met at the palace of Count Giovanni de' Bardi for discussions about the music of ancient Greece and its fabled capacity to stir the emotions.

Born in 1567, the same year as Saint Francis de Sales and one year before Saint Aloysius Gonzaga, Claudio Monteverdi grew up in Cremona, Italy, center of the greatest school of violin making—the school of Amati, Guarneri, and Stradivari. Along with his brother, Giulio Cesare, Claudio received his musical education from the esteemed composer Marc'Antonio Ingegneri, *maestro di cappella* of Cremona's cathedral. By 1582 Claudio already had an anthology of three-voice motets published by the Venetian publisher Gardane. In about 1590 he joined the musical staff at the ducal court of Mantua. The duke, Vincenzo I Gonzaga, was the head of the main branch of the powerful Gonzaga family.[1]

Duke Vincenzo's music director was the influential Flemish composer Giaches de Wert (1535–1596), who became musical role model for the young Monteverdi. Upon de Wert's death in 1596, another musician who had seniority, succeeded him, and Monteverdi would wait till 1601 for promotion to this post. Nevertheless, this did not impede Monteverdi's career, for so popular was his third book of madrigals that it was reprinted in 1594, but this was his last publication until 1603. During this time Monteverdi's reputation grew in Mantua and elsewhere, and in 1599 he married court singer Claudia de Cattaneis. The couple had three children, two sons and a daughter, of whom the sons—Massimiliano and Francesco—survived.

In 1600 the theorist and canon Giovanni Maria Artusi published an attack on what he considered unwarranted harmonic innovations in Monteverdi's music, citing madrigals that were as yet unpublished, for example, *Cruda Amarilli* (*Cruel Amaryllis*). Such notoriety was beneficial to Monteverdi's career and identified him as a modern composer who sought to heighten the expressiveness of the lyrics through daring harmonies. The works cited by Artusi later appeared in Monteverdi's fourth and fifth books of madrigals, published in 1603 and 1605. Book 5 also contained his draft of a riposte to Artusi, which was later published by Giulio Cesare Monteverdi. The Monteverdis argued that conventional counterpoint and harmony (typified by the imitative polyphony of such Renaissance masters as Palestrina, Victoria, and Byrd), which they called the *prima prattica*, were to be revered, but that Claudio's innovations represented something new—the

---

1   Saint Aloysius Gonzaga was a member of a junior branch of this family.

seconda prattica—in which music serves the words. Artusi's critique forced Monteverdi to articulate his new philosophy of the primacy of words over music! Now composers could move the passions, stir the emotions in a more powerful, rhetorical way through a solo vocal line accompanied by harmonies that could freely change to suit the meaning of the words.

After the Artusi episode another landmark was the premiere, in February 1607, of Monteverdi's *L'Orfeo*—the first truly great opera—at Mantua for the pre-Lenten carnival season. Earlier operas by Giulio Caccini and Jacopo Peri on the theme of Orpheus and Eurydice had introduced the new *stile recitativo*—or recitative style—in which a solo singer declaimed speechlike melodies over a simple chordal accompaniment. Monteverdi also cultivated this style but made it even more expressive and he enriched *L'Orfeo* as a whole by the introduction of more arias, choruses, and dancing.

It is fitting that several of the earliest operas presented the story of Orpheus and Eurydice, which is, after all, about the power of music. Caccini and Peri, guided by Count Giovanni de' Bardi and the gentlemen *literati* of the Florentine Camerata, sought to re-create in the music of their own time the marvelous emotional effects of ancient Greek drama, which they believed to have been completely sung. Caccini pioneered the new vocal style known as monody—a solo song with simple chordal accompaniment, usually played by a harpsichord (cembalo) or theorbo (a bass lute with a very long second neck). In 1601 Caccini published some of these monodies in the watershed volume *Le nuove musiche*. Both he and Peri composed the first operatic settings of the story of Orpheus and Eurydice. While Caccini's version was published first, Peri's version received the first performance at the wedding of King Henry IV of France and Maria de' Medici, held at Florence's Palazzo Pitti on October 6, 1600. Because of this happy occasion, Peri's librettist, Ottavio Rinuccini, took poetic license and gave the story a happy ending. As in Ovid's version of the story, Orpheus goes directly to Hades after his bride's death, and does not encounter *en route* any of the fabled individuals, such as Charon and Cerberus, mentioned in other versions. The bulk of Peri's *Euridice* features his new recitative style (*stilo recitativo*), which is speechlike singing. There were also arias, choruses, and dancing. Monteverdi's *Orfeo* uses these same elements but differs in certain ways.

L'Orfeo begins with a Prologue sung by *La Musica*—music personified—who sings of the power of music and announces the story of Orpheus and Eurydice. Act I is set before the wedding; Orpheus and Eurydice sing of their joy at their approaching nuptials, and a chorus of shepherds and nymphs sing and dance while invoking Hymen, the god of marriage. At the beginning of Act II, Orpheus sings to the shepherds a spritely aria celebrating his joy ("Vi ricordi, o boschi amorosi") ("Do you recall, o shady woods"), but they are interrupted by a messenger who announces the death of Eurydice, who was bitten by an asp. Orpheus, grief stricken, reacts with the expressive recitative "Tu sei morta" (You are dead), which tellingly depicts his numbness and disbelief at the death of his wife. In Act III Monteverdi's librettist, Alessandro Striggio, included Orpheus' encounter with the ferryman Charon (Caronte) at the gates of Hades, and this is really the centerpiece of the opera. *La Speranza* (Hope) guides Orpheus to the portals of Hades. As she leaves him on his own, *La Speranza* quotes the famous line from Dante's *Inferno*: "Abandon hope all ye that enter." Charon (Caronte) forbids Orpheus to cross the river but the grieving husband sings the aria *Possente spirto* (Powerful spirit) and pleads with Charon, flattering him in three impassioned and vocally ornate stanzas.[2] In each stanza Orpheus is accompanied by a different pair of instruments—violins,

---

2   The poetic form is *terza rima*, used by Dante in his *Divine Comedy*.

cornetti, and double harp (*arpa doppia*). Charon is not moved by Orfeo's singing, so he plays his lyre, which calms the ferryman and puts him to sleep. Orfeo then takes Charon's boat and crosses the river to Hades. The rest of the story proceeds familiarly except for the previously mentioned happy ending.

On September 10 of that year, Monteverdi's wife died. Claudio was inconsolable and postponed returning to work at Mantua, but eventually he had to get back there for the production of his opera *Arianna*. The year 1610 saw the publication of Monteverdi's *Vespers of the Blessed Virgin*. The volume actually contains, along with a musical setting of Vespers, a complete six-voice Mass and some sacred concertos. These three different components illustrate Monteverdi's Janus-like position in music history because they represent both conservative and progressive traits. The Mass, based upon a motet by Nicolas Gombert (ca. 1495–ca. 1560), is the most old-fashioned, and features a dense texture of imitative polyphony, what Monteverdi had termed the *prima prattica*. The Gregorian psalm tones of the Vesper psalms are elaborated with polyphony and instrumental accompaniment, a forward-looking trait. The sacred concertos, motets for solo voices and small instrumental ensemble, are the most progressive, with characteristics most like the new genre of opera and secular vocal chamber music. These expressive and dramatic works are what the composer had termed the *seconda prattica*. The secular, theatrical quality of this music is most evident by the fact that Monteverdi, at the beginning of the Vespers—*Deus in adiutorium*—borrowed the music from the opening toccata, or overture, to *Orfeo*. It is not clear whether the volume was meant for use with a specific liturgical feast, or whether it was merely an anthology, from which the choirmaster could select music for use during any Vespers; scholars have offered several theories.

During this time Monteverdi was becoming increasingly disenchanted with the Gonzagas. His release finally came in

July 1612, after the death of Vincenzo Gonzaga, when the duke's son and heir Francesco dismissed Monteverdi. In August 1613 Monteverdi was summoned to Venice, where he successfully auditioned for the position of *maestro di cappella* of St. Mark's Basilica. San Marco was the parish of the doges, rulers of *La Serenissima Repubblica*. As chapel master to the doges, Monteverdi had reached the pinnacle of success, as Venice was considered to be the most powerful and progressive city in Italy, and perhaps in Europe. While at San Marco, Monteverdi had the choir sing not only his own music, but also music by sixteenth-century masters like Palestrina and Lassus, and music by his own chorister-composers, like Francesco Cavalli, Alessandro Grandi, and Giovanni Rovetta. These last two served successively as deputy *maestro di cappella* to Monteverdi, thus providing the composer with more time to answer requests for operas and for madrigals, like those in his forward-looking Book 7. Monteverdi also accepted commissions for music from religious confraternities of laymen, like Venice's Scuola di San Rocco.

From about 1630 to 1638, Monteverdi composed little, and sometime around 1632 the widower was ordained a priest. The opening, in 1637, of Venice's Teatro San Cassiano, the first public opera house, sparked the final phase of Monteverdi's creative life. After the 1640 revival of *Arianna*, the elderly Monteverdi composed three new operas, including *Il Ritorno di Ulisse in patria* (*The Return of Ulysses to His Fatherland*) and his final masterpiece, *L'incoronazione di Poppea* (*The Coronation of Poppea*). *Poppea*, which premiered in 1642 (the year before the composer's death), is based on historical incidents from Tacitus' *Annals of Ancient Rome*. It tells the story of the beautiful and ambitious Poppea, who maneuvers to become the consort of the emperor Nero. The nobility of Penelope in *Il Ritorno di Ulisse* contrasts starkly with the immorality of Poppea, who will stop at nothing to get what she wants. The opera's tale of adultery, murder, suicide, and unbridled ambition ends with an exquisite and triumphant love duet between Nero and Poppea. The realism of the opera's *libretto* is shocking in its modernity; musically, though, it is a *summa* of everything that had been successful for Monteverdi in his earlier operas. The seamless flow from recitative to melodic aria-like passages fostered a dramatic verisimilitude that is not always present in opera.

Why did the septuagenarian Monteverdi—now a priest—compose a work in which virtue does *not* triumph over evil? Musicologist Denis Arnold has offered one plausible explanation. "Certainly the smouldering, illogical, immoral and very human atmosphere could not have been produced except by a man who had been through the agonies of the Gonzaga court (we may suspect that there is more than a trace of Vincenzo in the cruelty of Nero). In that power to transcribe human experience into music lies the greatness of Monteverdi."[3]

---

3   Denis Arnold and Nigel Fortune, eds., *The New Monteverdi Companion* (London: Faber and Faber, 1985), 124.

11

Orpheus Britannicus and
the French Connection

This is a tale of two countries, France and Great Britain. In 1660 the monarchy was restored in England after the regicide of Charles I and after more than ten years of Puritan rule under the Protectorate of Oliver Cromwell. After the death of Cromwell in 1658, England was in a chaotic state, and it took military action by General George Monck, the Duke of Albemarle—who marched from Scotland with his army—to restore the monarchy. Charles II (1630–1685), who had been in exile in France since 1646, returned to rule.

Charles was only sixteen when he joined his Catholic mother, Henrietta Maria (youngest daughter of the French king Henry IV and Marie de Medici), in France, where she had formed a Royalist court in exile, which remained the center of Stuart resistance to the Protectorate until Charles II was restored to the throne. The queen had been in France since 1644; thus, when Charles was crowned king of England in 1661 he had already spent fifteen years in France and had thoroughly assimilated French styles—including music—that he had encountered at the court and chapel of his cousin and near contemporary Louis XIV (1638–1715). By the time of his coronation, Charles had re-founded both the Chapel Royal and the King's Musick, but as musical organizations employing the French style.

The re-founded Chapel Royal provided a "nursery" for a new generation of English composers, a generation that

adopted the French style demanded by the king. Captain
Henry Cooke—a musician veteran of the Royalist army—was
engaged to train the Chapel Royal choristers—a gifted group
of boys, including among them Pelham Humfrey, John Blow,
and Henry Purcell. But the star of this constellation was Purcell, who would later come to be called *Orpheus Britannicus*.

What was this French style that King Charles II had
encountered during his exile, and which he demanded to have
in his own music establishment? Purcell's contemporary, the
lawyer, writer, and amateur musician Roger North (1653–
1734), would recall that

> the King professed an "utter detestation of Fancys" [the imi-
> tative music for viol consort popular in the early 1600s] and
> preferred music where he could readily identify the meter—
> the "step tripla" being declared a particular favorite.[1]

The period of Charles' exile was the regency of Louis XIV's
mother, Anne of Austria.[2] When his father, Louis XIII, died,
in 1643, the young king was only five years old, so his mother,
aided by Cardinal Mazarin, took over the rule of France until
he reached the age of twenty-one.

Since the sixteenth century, one of the hallmarks of French
music had been the court ballet, and the French penchant for
ballet continued into the seventeenth century and beyond. Louis
XIV loved ballet to such a degree that he danced frequently
in court productions, including roles "in three of Molière's
comédie-ballets."[3] The dynamic dance rhythms of French ballet found their way into other areas of French music, including
opéra, instrumental music, and even sacred music. Louis' chief

---

1   Roger North, *Memoirs of Musick*, ed. Edward F. Rimbault (London: George Bell, 1846),
103–4.
2   Her spiritual director was Saint Vincent de Paul.
3   A *comédie-ballet* is a play featuring both music and dance.

composer was Jean-Baptiste Lully (1632–1687), who had been brought to France from Florence in 1646 as a page in the court of a French nobleman. Lully was only six years older than the king, so the two became friends and Lully climbed the ladder of success at court. In 1653 Louis appointed Lully court composer of instrumental music and director of *Les petits violons,* one of. the king's elite ensembles. In 1661, the year that Louis came of age, he promoted Lully to superintendent of music for the king's chamber and director of the *24 violons du Roi,* the king's most elite ensemble. It was during this exact span of years that Charles II of England lived in exile in France with his mother and younger siblings.

When Charles was restored, one of his first actions was to import a group of French musicians—a "*maître,*" a harp-sichordist, and a few singers—who were incorporated into the king's Private Musick and who also might have provided music for the Catholic liturgies of his wife, the queen con-sort Catherine of Braganza. Charles then emulated his cousin Louis by recruiting English musicians for his own 24 Vio-lins, and in 1661, he sent John Banister, a member of the 24 Violins, to France, in order to learn and comprehend the French style more thoroughly. In April of 1662 the king put Banister in charge of a new "Select Band" of twelve musi-cians, this time modeled on *Les Petits Violons.* There were also further collaborations between Charles II and other French, or French-trained, musicians, all of which resulted in a hegemony of French musical style in Restoration England. Starting in 1662, the composers in the Chapel Royal were commanded to compose church anthems in the French style, and the musicians of the king's 24 Violins were made avail-able to accompany the choir and soloists in this new music. On September 14, 1662, the London diarist Samuel Pepys recorded his impressions of a Chapel Royal service that he had attended: "Violls and other instruments [played] a Symphony between every verse of the Anthem; but the Musique more full then it was the last Sunday, and very fine it is."[4] His positive response was not shared by everyone, however. Another famous diarist, John Evelyn, wrote the following after attending a service in December 1662: "Instead of the ancient, grave and solemn wind music accompanying the organ, was introduced a concert of 24 violins between every pause after the French fantastical light way, better suiting a tavern, or a playhouse, than a church."[5] In around 1665, the king sent the prodigiously gifted Pelham Humfrey (1647–1674), one of his Chapel Royal choristers, to Paris, in order to assimilate the French style. This he did, along with the style of the Italian composer Giacomo Carissimi, whose music was also popular in France at that time. Tragically, Humfrey died at age twenty-seven, but even during his short life was able to influence the music of his slightly younger contemporaries John Blow (1649–1708) and Henry Purcell (1659–1695).

Purcell's verse anthem "My beloved spake" is a good example of the French influence on English sacred music.[6] The anthem begins in triple meter, with a snappy, dotted-rhythm, dance-like orchestral introduction/symphony that alternates with the solo quartet and the choir, as described above by Pepys and Evelyn. This is quite different from the "solemn" polyphonic anthems of William Byrd and even of Purcell himself, for not all of his church music is of "the French fantastical light way." Compare this to Lully's grand *Te Deum*, which also features alternation between solemn and dance-like styles, and between orchestra, solo quartet, and choir.

---

4   Richard Braybrooke and Mynors Bright, eds., *Diary and Correspondence of Samuel Pepys*, vol. 2 (New York: Dodd, Mead & Co., 1885), 336.
5   William Bray, ed. *The Diary of John Evelyn* (London & New York: Frederick Warne Co., 1889), 291.
6   A setting of Song of Songs 2:10–13, 16 (KJV) for a solo vocal quartet of alto/countertenor, tenor, and two basses and SATB choir.

One of the signature genres of French Baroque music is the *ouverture*, or French overture, which originally was meant to accompany the entrance of the king prior to the beginning of an opera. About a century later than Lully, Jean-Jacques Rousseau, in his *Dictionary of Music*, would describe this genre/style:

> The overtures of the French operas are almost all modeled on those of Lully. They are composed of a slow piece called *grave*, which is generally played twice, and of a tripping section called *gaie*, which is commonly fugued: several of these sections return to the *grave* at their conclusion as well.[7]

Lully began composing them for his ballets, beginning in 1658, and later his operas, and the French overture became a much-emulated standard of French Baroque music, well into the eighteenth century, by composers in other countries. Both J. S. Bach and Handel (for *Messiah*) composed French overtures, or passages in the French overture style, and Henry Purcell also incorporated the French overture into his music.

In addition to Anglican church anthems, Henry Purcell composed much incidental music for plays, as well as an opera—*Dido and Aeneas*—and theatrical works known as semi-operas (e.g., *The Fairy Queen* and *King Arthur*). These last works feature spoken dialogue, whereas *Dido and Aeneas* is the composer's only opera, a theatrical work that is sung throughout.

Purcell's *Dido and Aeneas* exhibits both French and English characteristics. The opera opens with a brief majestic French overture. The plot is based—somewhat loosely—on Book 4 of

---

7   Jean-Jacques Rousseau, *A Complete Dictionary of Music*, trans. William Waring, 2nd ed. (London, 1779), 305. Corrected and revised on the basis of the French original, quoted in Piero Weiss and Richard Taruskin, eds., *Music in the Western World: A History in Documents*, 2nd ed. (Belmont, CA: Schirmer Cengage Learning, 2005), 242.

Vergil's *Aeneid*. Purcell engaged the poet and Anglican clergy-man Nahum Tate to create a libretto, and Tate made several changes from Vergil's original. In the *Aeneid* the source of the main conflict in the tale is the goddess Juno's resentment of the Trojans. In Book 4, when Aeneas and his men reach Carthage, he meets Dido, the queen, and tells her the story of his wanderings. Dido falls in love with Aeneas, and the evil genius Juno arranges with Venus (the mother of Aeneas) for him to respond to Dido's love in order to distract him from his destiny of founding Rome. After their (presumed) night of love, Jupiter sends Mercury to Aeneas to remind him of his mission. In Tate's retelling of the story, an evil sorceress and her "enchantresses" conspire to destroy Carthage. They hate Dido and dispatch their "trusted elf," disguised as Mercury, to convince Aeneas to abandon Dido and sail on to Italy. The *faux* Mercury will surely have the authority to persuade Aeneas to leave Dido; the sorceress and her infernal crew break out in sung ghoulish laughter.

Modern scholarship has suggested that Purcell's opera is a political allegory. Tate's libretto is based on his 1678 play, *Brutus of Alba*, or *The Enchanted Lovers*, which also contains the story of Dido and Aeneas. The play's prologue mentions the delight when two monarchs wed, which could refer to William and Mary. Also, in a poem from the mid-1680s, Tate equates James II with Aeneas, whom the sorceress and her enchantresses (symbolizing Catholicism, a conventional analogy of that era) deceive into abandoning Dido, a metaphor for the British people. This would account for Tate's addition of the sorceress and her witches.

One particularly English element in Purcell's opera is the air that opens the third (and final) act. As Aeneas' fleet prepares to leave the port of Carthage, a lone sailor sings, "Come away, fellow sailors," answered by the chorus of his mates. It is in the jaunty style of a triple-meter hornpipe, but this is a polar opposite to the opera's denouement, when Dido, lamenting the departure of Aeneas, sings the noble, and justly famous, recitative and air "Thy hand, Belinda ... When I am laid in earth." The musical foundation of this air is a ground bass, which is a constantly repeating melody in the bass line, over which Dido's melody floats. The descending pattern of the ground bass was standard in the seventeenth century as a metaphor for lament, but Purcell augments and embellishes his ground bass melody. Who can forget her repeated "Remember me, but, ah, forget my fate," as Dido prepares to immolate herself? After her death the chorus, tenderly but solemnly, enjoin "cupids to scatter roses on her tomb, soft and gentle as her heart. Keep here your watch, and never, never part."

Purcell's *Dido and Aeneas* has so many musical and dramatic riches, yet it is only about an hour long. The only reported performance took place in 1689 at Josias Priest's girls' school, in Chelsea, at that time a village to the west of London. Were all the roles sung by the girls? There is still much we do not know for sure about this brief opera, but it continues to delight and move hearts even today.

12

"The Red Priest"

La Serenissima Repubblica was on the cusp of its last century—
the eighteenth—when Antonio Vivaldi was born. The Most
Serene Republic ended in 1797, when Venice was awarded to
Austria by Napoleon and his conquering armies. The century
saw a final blaze of artistic glory for Venice, and Antonio Vivaldi was one of her most brilliant luminaries.

The composer's father, Giovanni Battista Vivaldi, known
as Rossi because of his red hair, was a violinist at St. Mark's
Basilica when on March 4, 1678, his first child was born.
Antonio inherited his father's red hair; thus, the younger
Vivaldi came to be called *Il prete rosso*, the "red (headed)
priest." Antonio also inherited his father's musical gift and
as an eighteen-year-old was recruited as an extra violinist for
Christmas at San Marco. Already, though, since September
1693, Antonio had been training for the priesthood, and in
1703 he was ordained. After about a year, however, Don
Antonio ceased celebrating Mass, although he continued
as a priest. Years later he would say that a "tightness" of
chest (perhaps asthma) caused his withdrawal from liturgical duties.

In 1703 Vivaldi began his association with the *Pio Ospe-
dale della Pietà*, an orphanage for girls, usually known simply
as the *Pietà*. Founded in 1346, it was one of four Venetian
orphanages offering music instruction. Frenchman Charles de
Brosses described these institutions after a visit to Venice.

The transcendent music is that of the *ospedali*. There are four of these, made up of illegitimate and orphaned girls and those whose parents are not in a position to raise them. They are brought up at the expense of the state and trained solely to excel in music. They sing like angels and play the violin, the flute, the organ, the oboe, the cello, and the bassoon.... They are cloistered like nuns.... About forty girls take part in each concert.[1]

At concerts the girls performed behind a grille; in his *Confessions* Jean-Jacques Rousseau was moved to write, upon hearing them:

> I have not an idea of anything so voluptuous and affecting as this music; the richness of the art, the exquisite taste of the vocal part, the excellence of the voices, the justness of the execution, everything in these delightful concerts concurs to produce an impression which certainly is not the mode, but from which I am of opinion no heart is secure. [2]

Vivaldi was hired as *maestro di violino*. During the next years his first two collections of sonatas were published; in 1711 came Opus 3, a collection of concertos called *L'estro armónico* (*Harmonic Inspiration*), which marked the beginning of Vivaldi's illustrious career as a composer. Don Antonio was active as a composer of sacred choral music and opera, but his greatest contribution was in the further development of the concerto, a musical genre that was fairly new at the time.

Instrumental music as a separate art had begun to blossom in the sixteenth century, but by the early 1700s it was flourishing and capturing the imagination of composers and

---

1   Quoted in Daniel Heartz, *Music in European Capitals: The Galant Style, 1720–1780* (New York: W. W. Norton, 2003), 180–81.
2   Jean-Jacques Rousseau, *The Confessions of Jean-Jacques Rousseau* (London: Aldus Society, 1903), https://www.gutenberg.org/files/3913/3913-h/3913-h.htm.

the public. Advancement in the construction of string instruments, especially those made in Cremona by Amati, Guarneri, and Stradivari, assisted greatly in the evolution of a new instrumental genre—the concerto—for solo instrument (or instruments) and orchestra. The remote origin of the concerto lies in Catholic liturgical music; the term *concerto* had a flexible meaning throughout the seventeenth century. In the early seventeenth century the adjective *concertato* (concerted) meant "accompanied by instruments" and its etymology was from the Italian, "to agree with." The genre began in Italy, with Italians composing sacred concertos both for large choirs and instrumental ensembles as well as for small ensembles of one or two singers accompanied instrumentally, usually by a theorbo (bass lute) or organ and bass viol. Secular vocal music (e.g., madrigals) also adopted *concertato* style, and as the seventeenth century proceeded, *concerto* came to mean music for instrumental ensemble.

By the end of the seventeenth century, composers had begun to write music for instrumental soloist (or soloists) accompanied by orchestra. When there is more than one soloist you have a *concerto grosso*, a "large concerto." This *opposition* of soloist(s) to orchestra now justified using the *Latin* definition of *concertare*, "to vie with."

The basic form of a concerto is the alternation between a *ritornello* and a number of solo episodes. The *ritornello* (little return) is played by the full orchestra—*tutti*—and its melody represents a mood, or "affect," which anchors the form and gives the listener an element of repetition and stability. Between the repetitions of the *ritornello*, the soloist plays episodes of fantastic figuration.

Vivaldi's predecessors, notably, Arcangelo Corelli and Giuseppe Torelli, were the pioneers of the concerto, but in his 450-plus concertos Vivaldi enriched the genre exponentially. Most of his concertos feature a solo violin, but he also composed concertos for other instruments. Although Vivaldi composed so many concertos, we shall see in *The Four Seasons* how he kept his inspiration fresh and imparted variety to his concertos.

In 1725 Vivaldi published a new set of twelve violin concertos, *Il cimento dell'armonia e dell'inventione* (*The Contest between Harmony and Invention*). Concertos 1–4 were titled *La primavera, L'estate, L'autunno,* and *L'iverno,* the names of the four seasons. In *The Four Seasons* Vivaldi's originality is displayed in a unique and pioneering way. Each of the four scores has a sonnet with it that narrates aspects of each season. Thus, Vivaldi intended his music to describe what is being narrated, and in each score relevant lines from each sonnet are placed over the spot in the score where the action being described occurs. This is an early example of pictorialism, or program music, the depiction in music of extra-musical events and ideas; it's a genre that would not be fully realized until the nineteenth century with composers like Berlioz and Liszt.

Typical of most concertos, *Spring* (*La Primavera*) has three movements; the first and third are fast and the second is a contrasting slow movement. *Spring* begins with the full orchestra (*tutti*) playing a "bouncy" *ritornello* in E major, the concerto's key. The soloist imitates—through short notes decorated with trills—chirping birds, and above the staff the sonnet describes the birds greeting spring "with happy songs." After a shortened *ritornello* the orchestra imitates with oscillating sixteenth notes the flowing streams and "quiet, happy breezes." Again there is a shortened *ritornello*, but in a new key, B major. Suddenly the violins play rapidly repeated notes and fast, ascending scales announcing the approach of a thunderstorm. The soloist has furious passages of jagged sixteenth-note triplets, suggesting lightning. There is a shortened *ritornello*, now in C-sharp minor. The soloist plays, still in C-sharp minor, accompanied by a sustained C-sharp in the bass, but suggesting the renewed singing of the birds, mentioned above the staff. This indicates the subsiding of the storm; finally, the birds return, chirping merrily in the original key, E major. The middle movement is delightfully picturesque. Traditionally, a concerto's middle movement features a pared-down orchestral texture, often without bass, and an aria-like, embellished solo. In *Spring* this movement depicts a sleeping goatherd, guarded by his watchdog, under a tree. Violins I and II play oscillating dotted-note figures to represent "leafy branches rustling overhead," while the soloist represents the goatherd. Underneath these three staves is text identifying the viola line as "il cane che grida," the barking dog. The viola repeats a single pitch in short, sharp rhythms to simulate the dog's barking. The final movement portrays rustic dancing by nymphs and shepherds accompanied by a bagpipe. The bagpipe's drone is played in sustained notes by viola and bass at the interval of a fifth, which suggested to Vivaldi's audience the *zampogna*, or rustic Italian bagpipe. Above these instruments the soloist represents both the bagpipe's chanter and the dancing with a lively 6/8 meter.

Summer (*L'Estate*) is in G minor and is a musical portrayal of sultry heat. Vivaldi includes bird calls and another storm, this one more violent than the spring storm. Rather than a straightforward *allegro* throughout the first movement, the *ritornello* begins "Allegro non molto" (Not too fast), in 3/8 meter. Each measure begins with a rest, suggesting a limping gait. But there is constant alternation between this languorous style and an animated style that mimics various birds and atmospheric states. We hear stylized cries of various birds (cuckoo, turtle dove, goldfinch) who sense the approaching storm. The cuckoo is portrayed by the soloist, represented by fast passages of sixteenth notes in 4/4. The characteristic descending minor-third "call" of the cuckoo is embedded in the sixteenth-note figures. Now comes a shortened *ritornello* followed by another solo episode, this time representing the turtle dove with its soft cooing, and the finch, which has a livelier song. Now Vivaldi introduces a longer *tutti* passage that does not use the *ritornello* theme. It depicts a gentle breeze followed by the "threatening North Wind," and then a five-measure segment of the *ritornello*. The next solo episode portrays the cry of the shepherd at the approaching storm. The movement ends with the full fury of the storm and no *ritornello* theme!

The middle movement is characteristically short and depicts the shepherd waking from his "rest." Underneath the solo violin are repeated, percussive, dotted notes representing flies and hornets, and a single repeated pitch representing thunder. The *ritornello* of the third movement uses the same material found in the latter part of the first movement, thus reprising the thunder; the third movement is the storm itself.

Autumn opens with raucous revelers celebrating the harvest. The *ritornello* is in 4/4 with heavy accents on the first and third beats, illustrating the sturdy dancing of peasants, while the solo violin depicts the unsteady gait of rustics who have drunk too much wine and eventually fall asleep.

The *Adagio* portrays the peasants' slumber; here the soloist merely doubles the first violins. In the third movement hunters appear in the opening *ritornello*, signaled by a leaping melodic figure representing hunting horns. The soloist's first episode also imitates horn calls through the use of arpeggios. After the third statement of the *ritornello*, the soloist becomes the prey and the *tutti* the hunters. As the hunt progresses, the soloist's figuration (e.g., scales) quickens. Finally, at the last solo episode, the slow tempo signifies that the prey has been wounded. The last, trilled cadence of the violin solo signifies the death of the prey. The full *ritornello* is played one last time.

The jovial F major of *Autumn* now yields to minor as *Winter* begins with repeated eighth-note figures that suggest "freezing and shivering" (or even teeth chattering). Vivaldi's harmonies set our teeth on edge with their dissonance. The solo violinist plays rapid thirty-second note scales and arpeggios suggesting the gusty, frigid winds. At the words "Running and stamping one's feet," Vivaldi introduces a new *ritornello* theme in which the repeated eighth notes are exchanged for the smaller note values of sixteenth and thirty-second notes. We perceive this as faster, even though the tempo is the same. Now the soloist ("the wind") takes off with thirty-second note scales. A shortened *ritornello* appears, followed by another solo episode, illustrating chattering teeth. Finally, the movement ends with the "second" *ritornello*.

Winter is not all bad; often we remember cozy scenes by the fire while rain patters against the window. This is what Vivaldi portrays in the middle movement. The key relaxes from F minor to E-flat major; the soloist plays a lovely, lyrical melody accompanied by *pizzicato* (plucked) strings. For the final movement Vivaldi introduces escapades on ice and he departs from *ritornello* form. It begins with a solo violin passage illustrating how carefully one navigates an icy path from fear of falling. The *tutti* continues in longer note values, illustrating the cautious, slow steps described in the poem. The movement depicts a fall on the ice, blustery winds, and ends with sequestration indoors.

The Four Seasons are a wonderful illustration of Vivaldi's inventiveness. They show how, although he contributed to the stabilization of *ritornello* form, he could still bend that form and depart from it.

13

The Restoration of Johann Sebastian Bach

A young man named Johann Adolph Scheibe (1708–1776), born and reared in Leipzig, moved to Hamburg in 1736. After teaching himself organ and failing to gain employment as an organist, he became a music critic and composer. As blogging had not yet been invented, Scheibe started *Critische Musikus*, a fortnightly journal of music criticism. In issue number 6 (May 14, 1737) an anonymous letter appeared. The writer, a certain "Able Musikant," attacked a renowned musician who, he admitted, was "an extraordinary artist on the clavier and on the organ," yet there was much blameworthy music composed by this musician.

The young man's critique reflected his taste for what was *au courant* in music. For men like Scheibe, born in the early eighteenth century, music had to have "amenity", that is, it must be pleasing, and it must be "natural." By "natural," Scheibe meant that a pleasing melody with a simple, discreet accompaniment was all-important, and that melody must dominate. Contrasted to this idea was the "confused," "turgid" style, darkened by "an excess of art," characteristic of the music of "the great man." All this refers to music with a learned, contrapuntal texture—the texture associated with fugues. In a fugue, no melodic line is dominant; all voices are equally important, and this was something that young Scheibe could not abide. When the "Able Musikant" (actually Scheibe himself) attacked the "great man" for expressing

101

"every ornament, every little grace, and everything that one thinks of as belonging to the method of playing, he expresses completely in notes," he meant that this composer wrote out the ornamental notes instead of letting the performer add them *ad libitum*. Scheibe's emphasis on such "noble simplicity" perfectly accorded with the burgeoning influence of the Enlightenment.

Even though he had adopted some features of the newer, more melodic style, J.S. Bach (1685–1750) was considered by Scheibe to be old-fashioned; Bach's music did not keep up with the latest trends. Perhaps that is one reason why, after his death, Bach's music was almost forgotten for many years. Of Sebastian's most famous sons, the eldest, Wilhelm Friedemann (1711–1784), continued to compose in both older and newer styles. Carl Philipp Emanuel, the second eldest (1714–1788), creatively reconciled both styles, while the youngest, Johann Christian (1735–1782), was completely of the new school and was himself an influence on Mozart.

After the death of Johann Sebastian Bach, only a tiny coterie of his students and aficionados kept alive appreciation for his music. Even at Leipzig's *Thomaskirche*, where Bach had been music director for twenty-seven years, his cantatas and organ music were not often performed. Occasionally, a pupil or one of his sons might play one of Bach's organ works, but for all practical purposes, Bach was remembered as an organ virtuoso or a pedantic contrapuntist. In 1782 the composer Johann Friedrich Reichardt (1752–1814) wrote that "had Bach possessed the high integrity and the deep expressive feeling that inspired Handel, he would have been much greater even than Handel; but as it is, he was only more painstaking and technically skillful."[1] Enthusiasm for Handel's music had

---

1   Quoted in Nicholas Temperley, "Bach Revival," *The New Grove Bach Family* (New York: W.W. Norton, 1985), 168.

never waned, possibly due to his generally more melodic style and the popularity of his operas and oratorios with a concert-going public.

A small flame for Bach's music was kept burning, however, and gradually it developed into a network of votaries. In Berlin, where Emanuel Bach was in the service of Frederick the Great until 1767, a small but influential group of disciples had formed. It was thanks to them that many of Bach's manuscripts were saved, and it was from here that the network expanded. The Viennese ambassador to Berlin, Baron Gottfried van Swieten (1733–1803), would transport copies of Bach's music back to Vienna, where the young Mozart would study the scores with admiration. Haydn, too, benefited from van Swieten's music library. This exposure to Bach's music inspired Haydn and Mozart to infuse sections—or even whole movements—of their works with counterpoint. The final movement of Mozart's Symphony No. 41 ("Jupiter"), for instance, is a fugue.

Ultimately, it took the nineteenth-century Romantic movement to be the catalyst that would restore Bach's music to its rightful place of honor and put him in the highest echelon of composers. One distinguishing characteristic of the Romantics was their nostalgia for the past. German Romantics, in particular, were seeking for all that was distinctively German and all that was best in their past, and this, combined with religious revival, led to a renewed focus on Bach as an icon of German Christianity. One writer who was tireless in promoting Bach in this way was Johann Nicolaus Forkel (1749–1818), who in 1802 published the first biography of Bach. Forkel dedicated it to Baron van Swieten and its inscription read: "for patriotic admirers of true musical art … This great man was a German. Be proud of him, German fatherland, but be worthy of him too.… His works are an invaluable national patrimony with which no other nation has anything to be compared."[2] Johann Friedrich Rochlitz (1770–1842), editor of the Leipzig journal *Allgemeine musikalische Zeitung*, believed that Bach kept company with Michelangelo, Rubens, Dürer, and Newton.

Meanwhile, Johann Philipp Kirnberger and Johann Friedrich Agricola, from the Berlin Bach circle, had presented an assortment of Bach's music to Carl Friedrich Zelter (1758–1832), another Berlin musician. Faced with this treasure trove, Zelter did what any music lover would have done; he took steps to have the music performed.

The crowning event, however, of the growing rehabilitation of Bach's reputation was the revival of his *Saint Matthew Passion* (*Matthäus-Passion*), in 1829, by Zelter and the Berlin *Singakademie*, conducted by twenty-year-old Felix Mendelssohn. This was the event that brought Bach fully back into public consciousness. More performances of the work followed, then performances of other large works in either full (*Saint John Passion*, 1833) or cut (Mass in B minor, 1835) versions.

Thus, Bach became the first great composer to have his reputation restored posthumously. Thanks to Zelter and Mendelssohn the *Matthäus-Passion* was revealed for the masterpiece it is. Despite the fact that Bach intended it for the Lutheran church, the Passion has deep Catholic roots.

The remote (i.e., Catholic) origins of Bach's *Matthäus-Passion* are the liturgical Passions of Holy Week, and they were not spoken—as is common today—but sung throughout. Traditionally, the Passion according to Saint Matthew is sung on the second Sunday of the Passion, Palm Sunday. Ninth-century descriptions of Roman liturgy mention that the Gospel accounts of Christ's Passion were chanted by one singer (*diakon*), but over time the number of chanters settled into three. The role of Christ is sung in the lowest vocal range. The Evangelist (narrator), who has the lion's share of chant,

2   Ibid., pp. 169–70.

is sung at a medium range, and all other roles (Peter, Judas, Caiaphas, a Maid, Pilate, and the crowd, or *turba*) are sung in the highest vocal range. Compared to Bach's Passions with their orchestras and choruses, this monophonic rendering by one voice might seem austere, but in a Catholic liturgical setting, the emphasis must be on the solemn declamation of the text. All four chant Passions are sung to a unique melody—or tone—that is exclusively used for Passions.

Starting in the fifteenth century, the Passions began to include polyphonic sections for the *turba*, so that their renditions would project a more realistic character.

Early Lutherans appropriated the Catholic liturgical practice of singing the Passions. In fact, they spread out the practice over both Passion weeks, with monophonic and polyphonic versions assigned variously to Matins and Vespers, as well as to Mass.

Since 1723 Bach had been director of music for all five Lutheran parishes in Leipzig; however, only the two largest had elaborate music. The first performance of his *Saint Matthew Passion* at Saint Thomas Church was probably on Good Friday of 1727. Bach, both in his church cantatas and his Passions, followed a practice that had become popular in his day; the texts of these works included three elements. Holy Scripture was supreme, and in the Passions most necessary (Bach used passages from Matthew, chapters 26–27), but added to it were tropes of the biblical text in the form of original poetry that furnished personal meditations on the scriptural text. Bach chose mainly the poetry of Christian Friedrich Henrici (pen name, Picander) for the lyrics of these meditational arias and their recitatives, as well as for opening and closing choruses. The third element was the Lutheran chorale (hymn). These melodies and their lyrics would have been familiar to parishioners at Saint Thomas and Leipzig's other Lutheran churches, and they were interspersed throughout the Passion. Bach presented some in their simple four-part harmonizations at various points in the *Matthäus-Passion*. Perhaps best known is *O Haupt voll Blut und Wunden* (*O Sacred Head Sore Wounded*). In addition, Bach used chorale melodies occasionally in solo arias and as a sort of "meta" melody in certain choral movements. For instance, in the opening chorus, *Kommt, ihr Töchter* (*Come, Ye Daughters*) of the *Matthäus-Passion*, the two choirs begin together: "Come, ye daughters, help me lament." They then call out to each other: "Behold! Whom? The Bridegroom. Behold Him! How? Like a Lamb," continuing in like fashion. Floating above this massive double chorus, a treble choir sings the chorale melody *O Lamm Gottes unschuldig* (*O Guiltless Lamb of God*). Bach uses a similar technique in *O Mensch, bewein dein Sünde gross* (*O Man, Bewail Your Great Sin*), the moving final chorus of Part I.

Bach's *Matthäus-Passion* is a work of such richness, depth, and variety that it is impossible to convey every facet of it in such a brief chapter, but perhaps a few highlights can provide an introduction. By the eighteenth century the musical style of the Passion had assumed many musical characteristics of Baroque opera, for example, recitative and aria. However, the sturdy chorales, and choruses with their contrapuntal texture, impart a sacred character. The Gospel narrative sung by the tenor Evangelist is in simple recitative, accompanied only by *continuo* (harpsichord and cello). Whenever Christ (a bass) sings, His words are uniquely accompanied by the orchestra's strings, which provide a "halo" around His sacred words. The arias, with their texts of poetic meditation, are accompanied by a variety of instruments that impart unique sound colors. For instance, Bach uses the poignant sound of a trio made up of a *flauto traverso* (flute) and two oboes *da caccia*[3] to accompany

---

3   The oboe *da caccia* (hunting oboe) is a member of the oboe family that is pitched a fifth below the oboe. Thus, it has a richer sound, somewhat like the *cor anglais*. It is distinguished by its curved body and brass bell.

the soprano aria *Aus Liebe will mein Heiland sterben* (*Out of Love My Saviour Is Willing to Die*).

> Out of love my Saviour is willing to die,
> though He knows nothing of any sin,
> so that eternal ruin
> and the punishment of judgment
> may not rest upon my soul.

This aria, and its preceding recitative, *Es hat uns alle wohlgetan* (*He Has Done Good to Us All*), follow the moment in the Gospel narrative when Pilate asks the crowd demanding Christ's Crucifixion, "Why, what evil hath he done?" The soprano contemplates Christ's sacrifice for her soul in a sinuous vocal line that bespeaks grief and sublimity. This is just one of many beautiful arias in Bach's *Matthäus-Passion*, but it has a particularly striking sound because of its unique instrumental accompaniment.

In his *Matthäus-Passion* Bach left behind the solemn chanted Passion of the Catholic liturgy, but his dramatic rendering of the Gospel affects listeners more dramatically. The freedom Bach exercised in blending chorale melodies, arias, and choruses with textual meditations on the Gospel is somewhat akin to the freedom used by Mel Gibson in *The Passion of the Christ*, his cinematic retelling of our Lord's Passion and Death. Gibson's fine work may be remembered a century from now, but Bach's masterwork will astonish and move for generations to come.

14

"Mr. Handel's Sacred Grand Oratorio"

Both J. S. Bach and Handel were born in 1685 in the state of Saxony. These two musical sons of Saxony, however, had very different careers. While Bach never left Saxony, Handel traveled to Italy and then, finally, to England, where he put down roots, becoming an English subject and changing his name from Georg Friedrich Händel to George Frideric Handel.

And how did Handel get to London? In 1702 he began studies at the University of Halle (his hometown) but seems not to have graduated. He then lived in Hamburg from 1703 to 1706, where he was a violinist and harpsichordist in the opera orchestra.

Handel's next destination was Italy, where he was based in Rome from 1706 to 1710. One musical highlight of this period was *Dixit Dominus* (1707), Handel's setting—for SATB chorus, soloists, and orchestra—of Psalm 110 (109), the first psalm of Sunday and festal Vespers. In typical Italian style of the early eighteenth century, each psalm verse is set for a different soloist or for chorus. It is easy to hear—thirty-five years early—*Messiah* in some of the music of *Dixit Dominus*, thus exhibiting Handel's genius and his debt to Italy. Other works from his Italian period were his oratorio *La resurrezione* and several operas, notably, *Agrippina*, which was a harbinger of Handel's bright future as an opera composer.

In 1710 Handel returned to Germany, where in June he began a job as music director to George, the elector of

Hanover, another German territory, near Saxony. Handel's contract stipulated a leave of absence—immediately—to go to London, so he left in July. While there he composed *Rinaldo*, his first opera for London, based on episodes from Tasso's epic *Gerusalemme liberata* (Jerusalem Delivered). *Rinaldo* was successful and established a good foundation for the trajectory of Handel's London career. The young composer left London for Hanover in July of 1711. In the fall of 1712, the elector gave Handel permission to travel once again to London with the understanding that he would return within "a reasonable time," but this is not what he did. By August 1, 1714, Handel was still in London and it was on this date that Queen Anne died. As the queen was childless, she was succeeded by the next in line, who happened to be George, elector of Hanover. Now that Handel's employer had become king of England, the composer would have to face up to having overstayed his leave. Despite several charming stories about Handel's *Water Music* and his reconciliation with George I, modern scholars doubt that Handel was ever out of favor with the king.

For most Catholics Handel is known as the composer of *Messiah*, but why did he start composing oratorios only after having composed about forty operas and much orchestral and keyboard music? Handel went from strength to strength as a composer of Italian opera, but not all Englishmen were enamored of it. As possessors of a great tradition of spoken drama, the English people had a "rationalistic Distaste for the Unnatural," which they considered opera to be. Joseph Addison wrote: "Our Country-men could not forbear laughing when they heard a Lover chanting out a Billet-doux, and even the Superscription of a Letter set to a Tune."[1] Another reason for English distaste for opera was the language barrier.

---

1   Joseph Addison, *Spectator*, no. 29 (Tuesday, April 3, 1711), https://www.gutenberg.org/files/12030/12030-h/SV1/Spectator1.html#section29.

Addison wrote in *The Spectator*: "There is no question but our Great-grandchildren will be very curious to know the Reason why their Fore-fathers used to sit together like an Audience of Foreigners in their own Country, and to hear whole Plays acted before them in a Tongue which they did not understand."[2] Subject matter was another complaint. The average Englishman was not interested in all those dead Romans, even though the educated classes were thoroughly conversant in ancient pagan literature. There was also an anti-Catholic streak: middle-class people saw Italian opera as a type of foreign "popery."

It was John Gay's *The Beggar's Opera*—a lighthearted story of characters in London's underworld—which in 1728 put the nail in the coffin of Handel's operatic career. After this he composed oratorios almost exclusively.

Oratorio is a full-length sacred music drama with soloists, chorus, and orchestra. It differs from opera in that it does not have stage action, sets, or costumes. The musical genre of oratorio has Catholic origins as it was initially a devotional service with song. This service was begun and promoted in sixteenth-century Rome by Saint Philip Neri and his Congregation of the Oratory. When Philip moved from his native Florence to Rome, he brought with him the popular *laude spirituali*, religious songs he had learned from his Dominican friar-teachers. It wasn't until between approximately the years 1620 and 1640 that the oratorio evolved from Neri's devotional service, at which simple *laude* were sung, to an extended musical genre that was more like an opera.

England never had oratorio until the eighteenth century, when it became very popular, solely thanks to Handel. There are several reasons why Handel's oratorios caught on in England.

---

2   Joseph Addison, *Spectator*, no. 18 (Wednesday, March 21, 1711), https://www.gutenberg.org/files/12030/12030-h/SV1/Spectator1.html#section18.

As noted above, Italian opera had fallen out of favor and a music theatre genre was needed that would fill the void and please the middle-class British public. The mid-eighteenth century was a time of prosperity and military success for England, and the British were able to find analogies between themselves and God's chosen people in the Old Testament. This was also an age of comfortable middle-class (Protestant) religion, and the Bible was a good storehouse of topics.

Handel's oratorios are not liturgical music; they are Christian entertainment and were often performed during Lent in place of opera. Most of them are dramatic oratorios in that they feature *dramatis personæ*, singers who represent the characters in the story. For example, in *Saul* (1738) Handel composed music to texts by Charles Jennens (1700–1773), to be sung by Saul, Jonathan, David, and Michal, to name just the most important characters.

Messiah, instead of being a drama about the life of Jesus, is a meditation of three parts upon the mystery of salvation. Jennens actually suggested the subject to Handel, and carefully selected passages from the King James Bible and the 1662 Anglican Book of Common Prayer to use for *Messiah*.

Clearly, Jennens was aware of the traditional (i.e., Catholic) interpretation of Holy Scripture, which comes from the Patristic writers. He was, in fact, a learned and fervent Christian, and a "stealth" evangelist. The years 1700–1750 saw the publication in England of a vast amount of poetry on the life of Christ and His divinity. Already, in 1712, Alexander Pope had written his own *Messiah*, a 108-line poem based on Vergil's Fourth Eclogue. According to scholar Ruth Smith, publication of these poems was motivated by three contemporaneous factors:

> a new enthusiasm for the Old Testament as a rich repository of sublime poetry; minute and exhaustive theological

discussion of the biblical texts traditionally taken to refer to
Jesus as the Messiah; and concern about the decline of religious feeling in England.[3]

Jennens' genius was that he saw the value of music, especially Handel's exalted and dramatic music, as a way to incul-
cate the Christian faith into a society that was becoming tepid
on account of spreading Enlightenment attacks on orthodox
Christianity and supernatural faith. Handel's musical gifts
and his years of experience as an opera composer served him
well in dramatizing Jennens' eighty-one biblical texts, ampli-
fying them in ways that permitted them to reach into listeners' hearts. The texts that Jennens chose were all passages that
would have been familiar; he rearranged them to tell anew the
story of salvation.

In the English-speaking world, Handel's *Messiah* has become
synonymous with Christmas, and indeed, its most often performed section is Part I, which follows a majestic French overture. Recall that Lully originally conceived the French overture
to accompany the king's entrance into the theatre.

Part I recounts the Old Testament prophecies of Christ's
coming, the announcement of His birth, and highlights of
His earthly ministry. The Old Testament books used for Part
I are Isaiah, Haggai, Malachi, and Zechariah, with the only
texts from the New Testament being a slightly adapted version of Matthew 11:28–30 (chorus: "His yoke is easy") and
Luke 2:8–14, the angel's announcement of Christ's birth, followed by the chorus "Glory to God."

Part II describes the Messiah's Passion, Death, Resurrection, and Ascension, as well as His preaching of the Gospel,
the world's rejection of it, and the eventual victory of God.

---

3   Ruth Smith, " '*Messiah*': *Realizing the Librettist's Design*," Notes to *Handel Messiah* (Gabrieli
Consort & Players/McCreesh). Archiv Produktion 453 464–2 (1997), 12–15.

It opens with the massive, fugal chorus "Behold the Lamb of God," words of Saint John the Baptist at Christ's baptism in the Jordan (John 1:29). The key is G minor, and the dotted rhythms suggest a French overture. Next is the air "He was despised," with lyrics from Isaiah 53, as are those of the following three choruses. Jennens chose the fourth of the "Suffering Servant" songs of Isaiah 53 for the depiction of the Man of Sorrows. To depict Jesus' agony on the Cross, Jennens adapted Psalms and the Lamentations of Jeremiah. Handel set three of these texts for tenor soloist. "All they that see Him" is an orchestrally accompanied recitative and is followed by the chorus "He trusted in God." These two numbers use text from Psalm 22 (21), which is traditionally used on Good Friday. Next is the tenor recitative "Thy rebuke hath broken his heart," which prefaces the arioso "Behold and see." How did Jennens and Handel depict the Messiah's Death and Resurrection? His Death is a brief orchestrally accompanied recitative, "He was cut off," another segment of the Suffering Servant song in Isaiah 53. The Resurrection is alluded to in the tenor air "But thou didst not leave his soul in hell," with words adapted from Psalm 17 (16). So, Christ's Resurrection is not directly stated and certainly employs no musical fanfares. This affecting air is followed by the sprightly F-major chorus "Lift up your heads," which is Handel's and Jennens' allusion to the Ascension. Here the lyrics are taken from Psalm 24 (23):7–10, and Handel takes advantage of their dialogue format by setting the words for divided chorus. The Messiah's identity is revealed in the following recitative: "Unto which of the angels said he at any time: Thou art my Son ...," and the subsequent chorus, "Let all the angels of God worship him." Both of these are from Hebrews 1, and the recitative also refers back to Psalm 2:7 ("Thou art my Son, this day have I begotten Thee"), which we encountered in Chapter 2. Part II ends with the "Hallelujah" chorus.

Part III is a meditation on the life of redemption, concluding with the sublime choruses "Worthy is the Lamb" and "Amen." The texts are all from the New Testament, except for Part III's opening air, "I know that my Redeemer liveth" (Job 19:25–26; 1 Corinthians 15:20). The lyrics of the next six numbers are also from 1 Corinthians 15. These passages depict the Resurrection life of the blessed in Heaven. The penultimate number is the aria "If God be for us"—encouraging words from Romans 8:31–34—and the glorious choral finale is "Worthy is the Lamb" (Revelation 5:9–14), with a fugal "Amen," as a grand coda.

On April 17, 1742, several days after the world premiere of *Messiah*, a reporter from the *Dublin Journal* enthused over the new oratorio.

> On Tuesday last Mr. Handel's Sacred Grand Oratorio, the MESSIAH, was performed ... the best Judges allowed it to be the most finished piece of Musick. Words are wanting to express the exquisite Delight it afforded to the admiring crowded Audience. The Sublime, the Grand, and the Tender, adapted to the most elevated, majestick, and moving Words, conspired to transport and charm the ravished Heart and Ear.

Handel himself conducted the first performance in Dublin—not London—as a benefit for several charities, and the premiere took place on April 13, not in December. *Messiah* was well received in Dublin, though Londoners warmed to it only gradually after its first performance there a year later, on March 23, 1743.

15

Joseph Haydn and the Princes Esterházy

The late eighteenth century in music has come to be known as the Classic, or Classical, era. This distinguishes it from the general definition of classical music. The "trinity" of composers associated with Viennese Classicism are Franz Joseph Haydn, Wolfgang Amadeus Mozart, and Ludwig van Beethoven. Of course, there were hundreds of other gifted composers in Europe—and even America—at this time, but it is these three who were singular in their contributions to the development of musical style, and their music epitomizes this gracious style in which art conceals art. To the pleasing and "natural" melodies of the early eighteenth century, the composers of the Classical era added many references to the "learned" or contrapuntal style that had been abandoned by J. S. Bach's sons and their generation.

In the life of Franz Joseph Haydn,[1] we see a man who rose from humble origins to world fame as a composer. By a combination of talent, hard work, and "luck," Haydn passed from peasant to choirboy to world-renowned composer.

Born in the eastern Austrian village of Rohrau, Joseph and his two younger brothers—Johann Michael and Johann Evangelist—had beautiful treble voices and were afforded the opportunity to attend choir school at Saint Stephen's

---

1   Joseph Haydn was born on March 31, 1732; George Washington was born on February 22, 1732.

Cathedral. Joseph was the first to go to Vienna; the Kapellmeis-
ter, Georg Reutter, was so captivated by his voice that he urged
Joseph's father to send his other sons. Michael followed, five
years after Joseph, and Johann Evangelist somewhat later.
Joseph's voice changed late, when he was about eighteen, so
he had to leave choir school. His parents did not have the
means to support further education, so Joseph struck out on
his own and a series of "coincidences" prepared him well for
the next stages in his life. He moved into an attic dwelling
next to Saint Michael's Church and began the life of a free-
lance music teacher, accompanist, and performer. As Divine
Providence would have it, nicer apartments on the floors below
Joseph's garret were inhabited by neighbors who would be of
great assistance to him. Joseph was able to receive free meals
from the Martínez family for instructing their daughter Mari-
anne (who would become a composer in her own right) in
singing and keyboard playing. Another resident of the same
building, and also a friend of the Martínez family, was Pietro
Metastasio, poet of the Imperial Court and the most famous
opera seria librettist. Last, but not least, through Metastasio,
Joseph met the famous singing teacher Nicola Porpora and
became his studio accompanist. Joseph was able to assimilate
much through being present at the Italian's singing lessons.
Haydn's earliest biographer, Georg August von Griesinger,
quotes Joseph as saying: "I profited greatly with Porpora in
singing, in composition, and in the Italian language."[2] What
he learned from Porpora filled the gaps in his choirboy musical education, and Porpora introduced Joseph to influential
people who could help him. In 1759 Joseph landed his first
regular job, as music director for Count von Morzin, but two
years later—on May 1, 1761—Haydn signed a contract for the
position of Vice-Kapellmeister to Prince Paul Anton Esterházy.

---

2   Quoted in Jens Peter Larsen, *The New Grove Haydn* (New York: W. W. Norton, 1983), 8.

The wealthy and powerful Esterházy family became Joseph's lifelong employers and catalysts in his career. Just under a year later Prince Paul died and was succeeded by his brother Nikolaus, known as "The Magnificent" for his lavish spending on the arts and for the building—in 1766—of Eszterháza, his country estate modeled on Louis XIV's Versailles. Prince Nikolaus, like his brother, was musical and constantly desired new music. In addition to symphonies and chamber music, Joseph also had to compose operas for Prince Nikolaus' pleasure. All of this furnished Haydn with a ready-made laboratory, as it were, in which he could experiment and develop as a composer away from the eyes of the wider world. As he was to say later:

> My prince was content with all my works, I received approval, I could, as head of an orchestra, making experiments, observe what created an impression, and what weakened it, thus improving, adding to, cutting away, and running risks. I was set apart from the world, there was nobody in my vicinity to confuse and annoy me in my course, and so I had to become original.[3]

And yet over time—despite his geographical isolation—word got out about the masterworks Haydn was composing in the wilds of Hungary and his music began to be published in Europe. In 1790, when Prince Nikolaus died, his son Anton succeeded him, but Anton did not share his father's love of music, so he dismissed the music staff. Nevertheless, Anton kept paying Haydn his usual salary. At this point, Haydn had been with the Esterházys for thirty years and was probably eager for a change, which Divine Providence provided with a momentous new venture.

---

3   G. A. Griesinger, *Biographische Notizen über Joseph Haydn*, trans. Vernon Gotwals, quoted in Larsen, *The New Grove Haydn*, 28.

Johann Peter Salomon, a violinist and concert impresario, had learned of Haydn's new freedom and approached him about the prospect of a tour to London. Salomon contracted with Haydn to compose six symphonies, an opera, and twenty smaller works. New Year's Day 1791 saw their arrival in London after a two-week trip, and Haydn marveled at the size and bustle of the city. London's citizens fêted Haydn and received him rapturously, as illustrated by this excerpt from Charles Burney's fulsome heroic couplets.

> Haydn! Great Sovereign of the tuneful art!
> Thy works alone supply an ample chart
> Of all the mountains, seas, and fertile plains,
> Within the compass of its wide domains.—
> Is there an Artist of the present day
> Untaught by thee to think, as well as play? . . .
> Thy style has gain'd disciples, converts, friends,
> As far as Music's thrilling power extends.
> Nor has great Newton more to satisfaction
> Demonstrated the influence of Attraction.[4]

So highly regarded was Haydn by Burney and (one assumes) Londoners, that he was compared to Isaac Newton and his law of gravity. London, seat of a constitutional monarchy, was a more modern city than Vienna—center of the Hapsburg Empire—and Haydn, servant of a prince, was treated with equality and with love by British citizens. While in London Haydn made many friends and stayed for about a year and a half. It is not surprising, then, that when Salomon proposed

---

4   H. C. Robbins Landon, *Haydn: Chronicle and Works, III: Haydn in England* (Bloomington, IN: Indiana University Press, 1976), 32–35, quoted in Piero Weiss and Richard Taruskin, *Music in the Western World: A History in Documents*, 2nd ed. (Belmont, CA: Schirmer Cengage Learning, 2005), 267.

a second trip, Haydn accepted, and for this trip (February 1794 to August 1795) he composed his final six symphonies. These, along with the six from Haydn's first visit, are collectively known as "London" symphonies, but his final symphony—No. 104—is also nicknamed "London Symphony." Haydn is often referred to as "Father of the Symphony" and "Father of the String Quartet" because he developed these genres significantly. The symphony, whose remote ancestor was the Italian opera overture (*sinfonia*), became one of the most popular musical genres of the eighteenth century, as witnessed by 12,350 surviving manuscripts. By the time Haydn traveled to London, he had already composed ninety-two symphonies, so he was thoroughly seasoned and sought to provide his audiences with new delights and inventive ideas at every concert. Several of his symphonies have nicknames (not bestowed by the composer); one of them is his Symphony No. 100, the "Military" Symphony. Like most symphonies this one has four movements: a fast movement preceded by a slow introduction, a slow movement, a minuet, and a very fast final movement. What innovations did Haydn use that made this symphony his most successful and that earned it the nickname "Military"? A music critic from the *Morning Chronicle* tells us as he gives an eyewitness account.

> Another new Symphony by Haydn was performed for the second time [April 7, 1794]; and the middle [i.e., second] movement was again received with absolute shouts of applause. Encore! encore! encore! resounded from every seat: the Ladies themselves could not forbear. It is the advancing to battle; and the march of men, the sounding of the charge, the thundering of the onset, the clash of arms, the groans of the wounded, and what may well be called the hellish roar of war increase to a climax of horrid sublimity! which, if others

can conceive, he alone can execute; at least he alone hitherto has effected these wonders.[5]

The anonymous journalist describes the militaristic qualities of the second movement; these are due to Haydn's unconventional use of triangle, cymbals, and bass drum, along with the usual timpani and a trumpet, which plays a bugle call (at the end of the movement). Additionally, Haydn makes much use of the brass (two horns, two trumpets) and woodwinds (flute, two oboes, two clarinets, two bassoons) for a very full and vivid "band" sound. For the audience these instruments would have conjured up the sound of a Turkish Janissary band with its percussion instruments whose use was unknown to Europeans before the midcentury fad for "Turkish" music. The eighteenth century witnessed the spread of fascination with non-European cultures; some other musical examples would be Mozart's opera *The Abduction from the Seraglio* (*Die Entführung aus dem Serail*) and the *Rondo alla turca*, from his Piano Sonata in A major, K. 331. In addition, very much on the minds of the audience would have been the ongoing French Revolutionary Wars, in which Britain was an ally against France.

Prince Anton died in 1794 and was succeeded by his son Nikolaus II, who reinstated the musical establishment at Eszterháza and brought back Haydn on a part-time basis. It was for Nikolaus II that Haydn composed the so-called *Lord Nelson Mass*, third in the series of six great Masses that Haydn composed from 1796 to 1802 for Princess Maria Hermenegild, his patron's wife. Each year the prince commanded Haydn to compose a Mass for his wife's Name Day, which

5   H. C. Robbins Landon, *Haydn: Chronicle and Works, III: Haydn in England* (Bloomington, IN: Indiana University Press, 1976), 247, quoted in Piero Weiss and Richard Taruskin, *Music in the Western World: A History in Documents*, 2nd ed. (Belmont, CA: Schirmer Cengage Learning, 2008), p. 269.

was September 8, the Nativity of the Blessed Virgin Mary. The *Lord Nelson Mass* was composed in 1798, in the midst of the Napoleonic Wars, hence the Mass' official title: *Missa in Angustiis* (*Mass in Troubled Times*). September 23, 1798, the day of the Mass' first performance, was almost two months after the August 1 victory of the British navy under Admiral Lord Horatio Nelson over Napoleon's forces in the Mediterranean Sea at Abu Quir Bay, off Egypt's coast; but word had not yet reached the Esterházy palace at Eisenstadt. Two years later, however, Lord Admiral Horatio Nelson and his party actually stopped at Eisenstadt for four days as they made their way back to London. Prince Esterházy lavishly fêted his guests, and during their visit Haydn's *Missa in Angustiis* was performed. Ever since then, this Mass has come to be known as the *Lord Nelson Mass*.

Some of the distinctive features of the *Lord Nelson Mass* are, first, the dramatic D-minor opening Kyrie, with its *bravura* soprano solo. This serious key returns in the Benedictus, where it imparts to the acclamations "Blessed is He who cometh in the name of the Lord," an ambience that is more appropriate to the Second Coming than to Christ's triumphal entry into Jerusalem on Palm Sunday. The Gloria and Credo are in a joyful D major, with the opening of the Credo featuring an ingenious canon. The Agnus Dei begins in G major, but Haydn rounds out the Mass by reprising D major. Because of wartime austerities, Prince Nikolaus had dispensed with his wind instruments, so Haydn creatively scored the Mass for strings, three trumpets, timpani, and organ. In the years left to Haydn, he composed his two oratorios, *Die Schöpfung* (*The Creation*, 1798) and *Die Jahreszeiten* (*The Seasons*, 1801), both of them inspired by Handel's oratorios.

On May 31, 1809, the frail seventy-seven-year-old Joseph Haydn died quietly in his own home in Gumpendorf, a Viennese suburb. June 1, the day of his burial, was the Feast of

Corpus Christi that year, and on the following day, a quiet Requiem Mass was offered at Gumpendorf's parish. Later, on June 15, a memorial service took place at Vienna's Schotten-kirche. This service, at which the music was Mozart's Requiem, was attended by many in Viennese society.

16

Wolfgang Amadeus Mozart

Wolfgang Amadeus Mozart is the second star in our Classical-era constellation of Haydn, Mozart, and Beethoven. Leopold Mozart had his son christened Joannes Chrysostomus Wolfgangus Theophilus because of his birthdate on January 27, the feast of the golden-mouthed Doctor of the Church. Sometimes Mozart went by Amadeus, the Latin version of the Greek Theophilus (friend of God, loving God, or loved by God); but more often he would use Amadé, Amadeo, or Gottlieb, the French, Italian, and German versions of the name. Mozart was a shining star in many genres of Classical music—symphony, concerto, piano sonata, sacred music—but opera is one in which his genius was especially effulgent.

Comic opera was an Enlightenment reaction against *opera seria*, a serious genre of opera that began to flourish in the early eighteenth century. *Opera seria* presented generalized characters and emotions, especially virtue, and it symbolized monarchy and Church. Comic opera was "a mirror of the Enlightenment," and national versions of it developed in different countries—*opera buffa* in Italy, *opéra comique* in France, *Singspiel* in Germany, and Ballad Opera in England.

Although early seventeenth-century Baroque opera had comic scenes, comic opera in the Enlightenment mold began to develop in the first quarter of the eighteenth century. In contrast to *opera seria* with its historical and mythological plots and royal or noble personages, comic opera had a simple story line and characters who were ordinary people, or even slapstick characters from the *commedia dell'arte*. Characters in *opera seria* would gesture nobly and stand still to sing, while in *opera buffa*, there was constant movement onstage. Indeed, comic opera followed the general Enlightenment penchant for what was considered "natural." In addition, comic opera, theatre, and literature all followed the contemporary vogue for the sentimental, which emphasized the emotions over rationality.

Mozart composed about twenty-three operas in all eighteenth-century operatic genres—including *opera seria*—but he is most noted for his comic operas, and here we shall focus on *The Marriage of Figaro* (*Le nozze di Figaro*), which premiered in Vienna just three years before the outbreak of the French Revolution. For his librettist Mozart engaged Lorenzo Da Ponte, who would also write librettos for *Don Giovanni* and *Così fan tutte*. Da Ponte adapted the recent, successful French comedy *The Crazy Day, or the Marriage of Figaro* (*La folle journée, ou Le mariage de Figaro*), by Pierre Beaumarchais. This play, because of its provocative political content, had not had an easy time with Parisian censors, but finally made its public premiere on April 27, 1784. And just what was it that made the play so provocative?

The story—comic, but serious elements—concerns Figaro and Susanna, two servants of the count and countess Almaviva. Both play and opera show the servants outwitting their master, the count, with the countess as an accomplice. *The Marriage of Figaro* is the middle play in a trilogy by Beaumarchais; it was preceded by *The Barber of Seville* (*Le barbier de Séville*) and followed by *The Guilty Mother* (*La mère coupable*). Readers will be familiar with *The Barber of Seville*, from the famous operatic setting by Rossini (and a less famous setting by Paisiello).[1] In the *Barber*, the disguised Count Almaviva,

---

1   *The Guilty Mother* (*La mère coupable*) had to wait until 1966, when its operatic version, by Darius Milhaud, premiered in Geneva.

with the help of his valet Figaro, elopes with Rosina, the ward of Dr. Bartolo. Years later, however, their marriage has become stale and the count is plotting infidelity to the countess (Rosina), namely, with Susanna, Figaro's fiancée. Susanna reveals this in the opera's opening duet, as she and Figaro are performing the mundane task of measuring the quarters they have been granted by the count. The entire opera takes place on their wedding day, and it is indeed a "crazy day" as several characters try to prevent Figaro and Susanna from getting married.

In Vienna, too, Beaumarchais' play had been censored, but many citizens were reading and discussing it, nonetheless. In the autumn of 1784 Mozart had acquired a copy of *Le Mariage*, and when he read it he realized it could become the libretto of an opera that would guarantee his success in Vienna. Mozart and Da Ponte approached an influential nobleman, Baron Wetzlar, for help in circumventing the imperial ban on Beaumarchais' play. Wetzlar volunteered to commission the opera, and if he was not successful in having the proscription lifted, he would arrange to have it performed in Paris or London. Ultimately, even though a German translation of Beaumarchais' play had been forbidden by Emperor Joseph II, he did grant permission for the play to be adapted as an Italian opera libretto. When making his adaptation Da Ponte condensed the number of characters from sixteen to eleven and the number of acts from five to four. He tightened the dramatic pace by shortening the dialogue (which would become recitatives). Lastly, Da Ponte deleted all political and many social references.

The Viennese premiere of *Figaro* took place on May 1, 1786. During the remainder of that year, *Le nozze di Figaro* was performed only nine times despite the first-night enthusiasm of the audience, and *Figaro* was considered to be not as successful as *Una cosa rara*, an opera by Vicente Martín y

Soler, a lesser composer. In November of that year, an Italian opera company in Prague produced *Figaro* to great acclaim, so Mozart and his wife traveled there in January 1787. In a January 14 letter to a friend, Mozart wrote: "For here they talk of nothing but *Figaro*. No opera is drawing like *Figaro*. Nothing, nothing but *Figaro*."[2]

Although *Le nozze di Figaro* has many memorable arias, these count for only half of the musical numbers. The rest consist of six duets, two trios, and one sextet; it is Mozart's ensembles that are the glory of *Figaro*. They allow for different emotions—of different characters—to be sung at the same time, a hallmark of ensembles, and especially the ensemble finale. It is the music that ties together the disparate emotions and enables the audience to grasp and follow the drama. Mozart ends Act I with Figaro's aria "Non più andrai," but there are ensemble finales at the end of acts two, three, and four. The ensemble finale developed earlier in the century, but Mozart's finales are extraordinary. In his memoirs Lorenzo Da Ponte described—two years prior to his first collaboration with Mozart—an ensemble finale in an opera by Salieri for which he was librettist.

> This *finale*, which must remain intimately connected with the opera as a whole, is nevertheless a sort of little comedy or operette all by itself, & requires a new plot and an unusually high pitch of interest.... Recitative is banned from the *finale*; everybody sings; & every form of singing must be available— the *adagio*, the *allegro*, the *andante*, the intimate, the harmonious & then—noise, noise, noise; for the *finale* almost always closes in an uproar.... The *finale* must, through a dogma of the theatre, produce on the stage every singer of the cast, be

---

2   Eric Blom, ed., *Mozart's Letters: Selected from The Letters of Mozart and His Family*, trans. Emily Anderson (Baltimore: Penguin Books, 1961), 221–22.

there 300 of them, & whether by twos, by threes or by sixes,
tens or sixties; & they must have solos, duets, terzets, sextets,
thirteenets, sixtyets . . .[3]

Figaro's Act II finale fits Da Ponte's description well. It
begins in 4/4 as an *Allegro* in E-flat with a churning accompaniment of broken chords. The enraged count and the fright-
ened countess have just returned—the count with crowbar
in hand—to open the wardrobe, in which the countess has
confessed that the mischievous pageboy Cherubino is hiding.
While they were gone, Cherubino emerged from the wardrobe
and Susanna, who had been hiding, took his place. The count
barks in dotted quarter and eighth notes while the countess
replies in swooning, wave-like, descending eighth-note figures.
The count draws his sword and demands that Cherubino come
forward from his hiding place. Suddenly the door opens, and
Susanna comes forth, to the surprise of the count and countess.
The full orchestra shrinks to just the strings; we can almost hear
a gasp as the count, and then the countess, exclaim: "Susanna?"
The music now changes to a stately, aristocratic minuet in B-flat.
Susanna explains that she was alone in the wardrobe and that
everything was a prank. The ladies explain that it was Figaro
who penned the anonymous letter (warning of a rendezvous of
the countess with a would-be lover) that Don Basilio brought
to the count. He begs her forgiveness, but Susanna and the
countess moralize about the affairs of men and women. Suddenly Figaro bounds into the room, thus turning the ensemble
into a quartet. The music changes to a lively triple meter in G
major; Figaro announces that musicians are waiting outside to
celebrate his and Susanna's wedding. Susanna, the countess,
and Figaro voice their fears *sotto voce* when the count says he

---

3   Lorenzo da Ponte, *Memoirs*, trans. Elisabeth Abbott (Philadelphia: Arthur Livingston, 1929),
133, quoted in Siegmund Levarie, *Mozart's Le Nozze di Figaro: A Critical Analysis* (Chicago: University of Chicago Press, 1952), 107.

wants to ask Figaro a question. After a pause, the count starts to pose his question over a C-major accompaniment (*Andante*, 2/4): he asks Figaro if he wrote the letter, which the count shows him. "No," Figaro replies; Susanna and the countess try to feed him words to explain the letter. He continues to evade the count but, just as Figaro and Susanna try to exit, the music suddenly modulates to F major. Now the ensemble expands to a quintet when Antonio the gardener rushes in and announces that a man has jumped down from the balcony into the garden and crushed the flowers. Antonio insists that the vandal was Cherubino, but Figaro casts aspersions on the gardener's veracity and claims the he, Figaro, was the one who jumped. Figaro, Susanna, and the countess try to malign Antonio as a drunkard, but he produces a paper he claims was dropped by the man. The count demands Figaro prove he was that man by identifying the document. Antonio exits and Susanna and the countess recognize the paper as Cherubino's military commission. The accompaniment changes to an *Andante* in 6/8 and the key of B-flat. This slower tempo helps prolong the suspense while Figaro—coached by the ladies—is trying to produce the correct answer. Eventually Figaro admits he was keeping Cherubino's commission—which fell from his pocket on jumping out the window—to give to the count because it lacked the count's official seal. However, no sooner has Figaro done this than an unlikely trio enter with designs to thwart Figaro's marriage. Dr. Bartolo, Don Basilio, and Marcellina bring accusations against Figaro. Now the tempo becomes a furious *Allegro assai*, the quintet becomes a septet, and the music returns to E-flat, the finale's original key. Because Figaro defaulted on a loan from Marcellina she is coming to claim the penalty—that he wed her.[4] Mozart divided the septet into two factions—a trio of the countess, Susanna, and Figaro, and a

---

4   Marcellina is Dr. Bartolo's housekeeper, and Don Basilio is the obsequious music teacher.

quartet with the count, Dr. Bartolo, Don Basilio, and Marcellina. Mozart tightens and relaxes the drama's pace through his planned progression of keys: E-flat–B-flat–G–C–F–B-flat–E-flat and also the use of different tempos, meters, and melodic types. This finale truly "closes in an uproar."

The Act III finale is the marriage celebration (not a nuptial Mass) of Figaro and Susanna, along with Dr. Bartolo and Marcellina, who have been revealed in the previous act to be Figaro's parents. Act IV's finale is set in the garden and portrays the duping of the count into meeting Susanna (actually, the countess in disguise) in the garden.

One facet of the remarkable genius of Mozart and his librettist Da Ponte is that they infused seriousness into a comedy. Beaumarchais' play has a lighter, more frivolous tone despite its political overtones, but Mozart's *Figaro*, in its satire on the aristocracy—the count and countess—shows them as both laughable and appealing. Figaro and Susanna, although servants, are depicted as intelligent and enterprising; in fact, Susanna's guiding hand can be discerned over everything. Mozart's music sparkles and wounds as we follow the humanity of the protagonists.

17

Ludwig van Beethoven

Ah, Beethoven—a man of paradoxes! Musicologists often dispute whether Beethoven should be considered to be a Classical or a Romantic composer, and music history books can vary according to these predilections. But even as we consider this epic—and transitional—composer, we can examine how Beethoven typifies these paradoxes, both in his music and in his era.

But here is another paradox. The Enlightenment is frequently described as an era promoting the advance of reason and the suppression of supernatural belief through a concerted effort to undermine "superstition" (Christianity and especially Catholicism). In the midst of the Enlightenment's rationalism—typified by the *Encyclopédie*—there is also a streak of emotion that is beyond rationalism: the recognition of the sublime. This can be seen in the writings of Edmund Burke (1729–1797), especially in *A Philosophical Enquiry into the Origin of Our Ideas of the Sublime and Beautiful* (1757), in the distinction he draws between the "beautiful" and the "sublime."

> For sublime objects are vast in their dimensions, beautiful ones comparatively small; beauty should be smooth and polished; the great, rugged and negligent ... the great ought to be dark and gloomy: beauty should be light and delicate; the great ought to be solid, and even massive. They are indeed ideas of a very different nature, one being founded on pain, the other on pleasure; and, however they may vary afterwards

from the direct nature of their causes, yet these causes keep up
an eternal distinction between them, a distinction never to be
forgotten by any whose business it is to affect the passions.[1]

In his 1813 essay, "Beethoven's Instrumental Music," the
polymath E. T. A. Hoffmann, in discussing the rise of instrumental music, discussed this distinction in his comparison of
the three greats of the Viennese School:

> That gifted composers have raised instrumental music to its
> present high estate is due, we may be sure, less to the more
> readily handled means of expression (the greater perfection
> of the instruments, the greater virtuosity of the players) than
> to the more profound, more intimate recognition of music's
> specific nature. Mozart & Haydn, the creators of our present
> instrumental music, were the first to show us the art in its full
> glory; the man who then looked on it with all his love and
> penetrated its innermost being is—Beethoven!
>
> The instrumental compositions of these three masters
> breathe a similar romantic spirit—this is due to their similar
> intimate understanding of the specific nature of the art; in
> the character of their compositions there is none the less a
> marked difference.
>
> In Haydn's writing there prevails the expression of a
> serene & childlike personality.... Mozart leads us into the
> heart of the spirit realm.... Thus Beethoven's instrumental
> music opens up to us also the realm of the monstrous and the
> immeasurable.[2]

---

1   Edmund Burke, *A Philosophical Enquiry into the Origin of Our Ideas of the Sublime and Beautiful* (London, 1757), quoted in Peter le Huray and James Day, eds., *Music and Aesthetics in the Eighteenth and Early-Nineteenth Centuries* (Cambridge: Cambridge University Press, 1981), 70–71.
2   E. T. A. Hoffmann, "Beethoven's Instrumental Music," (1813), in Oliver Strunk, ed. *Source
Readings in Music History* (New York: W. W. Norton, 1950), 775–77.

Clearly, for Hoffmann instrumental music was superior to vocal music and Beethoven was an exemplar of the sublime, which goes beyond the merely beautiful. Over the course of the eighteenth century, the importance of instrumental music had grown and almost supplanted vocal music. Rousseau, although a proto-Romanticist, opined that music without words was incapable of expressing moral ideas. Instead of relying on Aristotle's teachings on art "as an imitation of nature," writers noted the ability of instrumental music to express the emotions. Listeners to instrumental music were cast into the great sea of indeterminate emotion. Thus, the English writer and composer Charles Avison (1709–1770) could define the purpose of music thus: "to affect the passions in a pleasing manner, and as it uses melody and harmony to obtain that end, its Imitation must never be employed on *ungraceful Motions*, or *disagreeable Sounds.* . . . For Avison, then, music seemed to have no other purpose than aural pleasure."[3] His contemporary Charles Burney—eminent music historian, organist, and composer—wrote in his groundbreaking *General History of Music* that "[music] is an innocent luxury, unnecessary, indeed, to our existence, but a great improvement and gratification of the sense of hearing." These thoughts are a far cry from the ancient and medieval view of music as something of cosmic importance.

To listen to Beethoven's instrumental music is to be immediately aware of its more intense effect on the emotions, of its sublimity, its grandeur, and its nobility. Everything is raised up a notch with Beethoven! As it happens, there was an event in Beethoven's life that can be used to see how this is embodied, and it happened on just one night.

---

3   Charles Avison, *An Essay on Musical Expression* (London, 1753), quoted in Piero Weiss and Richard Taruskin, eds., *Music in the Western World: A History in Documents*, 2nd ed. (Belmont, CA: Schirmer Cengage Learning, 2005), 246.

Try to imagine yourself in Vienna at a marathon concert that included the world premieres of Beethoven's fifth and sixth symphonies, his fourth piano concerto (Op. 58, G major), and his *Fantasia*, in C minor (Op. 80, popularly known as the *Choral Fantasy*). These four works truly were premiered at the same concert, on December 22, 1808! The program of this four-hour-long concert consisted of the following works.

"Part I"

Symphony No. 6, Op. 68 ("Pastoral")
Ah, perfido! (Concert aria for soprano), Op. 65
Mass in C major, Op. 86—Gloria
Piano Concerto No. 4 (Op. 58, G major)

"Part II"

Symphony No. 5, Op. 67
Mass in C major—Sanctus/Benedictus
"Extemporized fantasia for piano"
Fantasia in C minor (Op. 80), known as the *Choral Fantasy*

Symphony No. 6—this is a programmatic symphony;[4] program music would become a major new genre in the nineteenth century, a Romantic calling-card, as it were. Beethoven's Sixth is popularly known as the Pastoral Symphony, and it has five movements instead of the more common four. The music of each movement depicts rustic scenes: *(1) Awakening of cheerful feelings on arrival in the countryside; (2) Scene*

---

4   Vivaldi's *The Four Seasons* (Chapter 12) was an early example of program music.

by the brook; (3) Merry gathering of country folk; (4) Thunder, Storm; (5) Shepherd's song. Cheerful and thankful feelings after the storm. The Symphony No. 5 (Op. 67) begins with what is probably the most famous melodic motive in history. The motive is four notes long but, incredibly, only made up of two pitches—G- and E-flat—but Beethoven masterfully develops the motive throughout all four movements of the symphony. The motive's rhythm—short-short-short-long—is likewise famous and is present throughout the symphony. The overall key of the symphony is C minor, though with A-flat major in the second movement. But Beethoven turns the tables by having the fourth movement—the finale—in C major. This turn from stormy C minor to triumphant C major has been noted by many commentators, and Brahms paid tribute to Beethoven by adopting the same key scheme in the first and fourth movements of his own Symphony No. 1. Beethoven's A-flat major second movement is lyrical and noble, a welcome relief from the furious intensity of the first. The third movement, the *Scherzo*, is fascinating as it does not fit the translation of *Scherzo* as "joke." The tempo, despite being labeled the typical *Allegro*, is a moderate triple meter. The rising intervals of the opening melody are played in a dynamic of *pianissimo*. The whole effect is one of mystery. The opening melodic motive alternates with a louder, more dramatic motive, which just happens to be in the same rhythm as the famous motive from the first movement. Near the end of the *Scherzo*, the dynamics once again soften, as if to end as they began, but Beethoven fools the listener. The *Scherzo* instead continues with a fragment of the opening melody; meanwhile, underneath, we hear in the timpani the famous rhythm of the first movment. Like a rocking chair the melodic motive seems set to go on *ad infinitum* until, with the change of one note (from E-flat to E-natural), it builds momentum and takes us directly into majestic and powerful C-major finale. It is truly an amazing moment!

Beethoven, of course, was the soloist in the premiere of his Piano Concerto No. 4 (Op. 58, G major). Although this concerto had had a private premiere in March of 1807, it had its public premiere at the "mammoth" December 22, 1808, concert. Unlike most concertos at that time, Beethoven's Fourth begins with the solo piano right from the beginning, instead of with an orchestral introduction. This opening solo is gentle in character, but as the orchestra enters and the movement progresses, there is a gradual expansion of sound; all in all, it is a movement of noble character. The slow second movement has a lament-like character with its E-minor key signature. The piano "speaks" in a dialogue with unison strings, suggesting the pleading of Orpheus with the Furies, according to Adolf Bernhard Marx, author of an 1859 biography of the composer. The movement ends very quietly, giving no suggestion of the spritely finale to follow. This Rondo is in C major, but eventually Beethoven takes the movement back to the concerto's original key of G major. Interestingly, there is a brief moment of D major, which features what sounds like a fleeting reference to the Ode to Joy melody from Beethoven's Symphony No. 9. That, however, was still seventeen years in the future!

Beethoven composed his *Choral Fantasy* specifically for this occasion as a kind of "grand finale" to the evening. The work, which is composed for piano, chorus, and orchestra, effectively united all the musical personnel who had been represented during the concert. Of course, Beethoven himself was the pianist, and at the premiere he improvised the opening solo of the *Choral Fantasy*.

Many have remarked upon the similarity of the "choral" theme in the *Choral Fantasy* to the "Joy" theme in Beethoven's Symphony No. 9. The composer himself described the

Ninth Symphony's famous choral finale in an 1824 letter as "a setting of the words of Schiller's immortal *Lied an die Freude* (Song to Joy) in the same manner as my pianoforte fantasia, but on a far grander scale."[5] The two melodies do have a similar contour.

The *Choral Fantasy* is in two sections—*Adagio* and *Finale. Allegro.* Eventually, Beethoven did write down the notes for the opening twenty-six-measure piano solo, and this comprises the *Adagio* section of the work. The *Finale. Allegro* section comprises the bulk of the *Choral Fantasy* and begins with a C-minor, march-like melody in the cellos and basses and some introductory flourishes by the piano. Eventually, about thirty-two bars into the movement, the piano begins the C-major "choral" theme. What follows is a succession of free variations showing off the pianist's virtuosity. Eventually, the four soloists, and then the chorus, enter with the "choral" theme, set to the words of a minor poet, possibly Georg Friedrich Treitschke (1776–1842). Pianist, chorus, and orchestra build up to a tremendous climax of this joyful dessert that topped off a menu of masterworks.

Post Scriptum: Beethoven was born just five years before Jane Austen, and his *Choral Fantasy* was actually performed in England during her lifetime. On February 22, 1815, there was a concert in Bath at which Jane Austen could have been present. The highlight of the second "act" of that concert was a performance of Beethoven's *Choral Fantasy*, which had premiered in Vienna only seven years earlier. The piano soloist on this occasion was the German pianist Friedrich Kalkbrenner (1785–1849), at that time considered to be Europe's most prominent pianist, who lived in London from 1814 to 1823.

---

5   Quoted in William Kinderman, *Beethoven* (Berkeley/Los Angeles: University of California Press, 1995), 132.

18

Romanticism in Music

A man stands atop a mountain; his back is toward us and he looks out at the vast array of fog-encircled mountain peaks ahead of him. This scene is depicted in *Wanderer above the Sea of Fog*, an 1818 painting by Caspar David Friedrich. Germany, an archetypal *locus* for Romanticism, may be the country where the term was first used in connection with music. E. T. A. Hoffmann, in his influential essay "Beethoven's Instrumental Music" (1813), wrote of instrumental music in general that "it is the most romantic of all arts—one might almost say, the only genuinely romantic one—for its sole subject is the infinite."[1] Hoffmann had used these words in several other essays, but here he applies them only to instrumental music. He felt that because instrumental music, unlike vocal music, had no connection with words, the meaning of the music was not predetermined by the text, but could express anything that the listener fancied. Interestingly, Hoffmann considered Mozart and Haydn to be Romantic composers, but for him Beethoven was the most Romantic. Of Beethoven's music he wrote that it "sets in motion the lever of fear, of awe, of horror, of suffering, and wakens just that infinite longing which is the essence of romanticism." One can see in Hoffmann's words "infinite longing" an example of the Romantic's exaltation of imagination and feeling over authority and rationalism.

---

1   E. T. A. Hoffmann, "Beethoven's Instrumental Music," (1813), in Oliver Strunk, ed., *Source Readings in Music History* (New York: W. W. Norton, 1950), 775.

Ernst Theodor Amadeus Hoffmann (1776–1822) was himself an embodiment of Romantic ideals. He was a lawyer, writer of supernatural tales, composer, conductor, and music critic, and he even exchanged one of his names, Wilhelm, for Amadeus, in homage to Mozart.

The Romantic era in music was an era of paradoxes. The uneasy relationship of music to words was resolved in program music, as represented by the new orchestral genres of program symphony, symphonic poem, concert overture, and incidental music. In these quintessentially Romantic genres, the music tells a story based on an extra-musical topic—for example, a poem or other literary work, a painting, or a scene in nature. Beethoven's Sixth Symphony ("The Pastoral") was a simple example in which the composer labeled each movement with a descriptive phrase, but his votary Hector Berlioz (1803–1869) carried the programmatic idea much further in his *Symphonie fantastique* (1830), by supplying a printed "program," which gave a detailed story of each movement and a melodic motive—which he called the *idée fixe* (obsession)—that represented the poet's beloved, or rather, his obsession with her.

In German *Lieder*, another new genre, the role of piano accompaniment was expanded, thus putting singer and pianist on a level playing field. Instead of composing music to order, composers began to compose for posterity; thus, the composer went from artisan to artist. On the one hand, the expanding bourgeoisie took up amateur music-making at home; on the other, the nineteenth century saw the rise of professional *virtuosi*, or "stars," like Paganini and Liszt. Romantics saw nature as an escape from the "dark Satanic mills" of the Industrial Revolution, and they likewise saw art as an escape, even to the point of some making art a replacement for religion. Another paradox was the expansion of the scientific method, while at the same time there was a turning toward the realm of the unconscious and the supernatural. This last can be seen as one way to fill the void left by the Enlightenment's abandonment of revealed religion for Deity and atheism. Little wonder, then, that literary works like Mary Shelley's *Frankenstein* and the works of Edgar Allan Poe became popular during this time. Romantic composers expressed themselves not only through their musical works but also through literary pursuits. Liszt and Wagner wrote essays; Berlioz and Schumann were musical journalists, with Schumann even starting his own journal *Die neue Zeitschrift für Musik*.

Beethoven notwithstanding, Franz Schubert is the first composer who can unequivocally be called a Romantic. In his brief thirty-one years, Schubert composed seven completed symphonies, much piano and chamber music, six complete Masses and many smaller sacred works, and over six hundred *Lieder* (one major new Romantic genre was the art song for voice accompanied by piano, known in Germany as the *Lied*, or plural, *Lieder*). Schubert's dramatic song *Erlking* (*Erlkönig*) epitomizes a number of stylistic traits of both Romanticism and the German *Lied*. Schubert set Goethe's poem *Erlkönig*, which has its roots in a Scandinavian legend. In Goethe's rendering of the legend, the Erlking (or Elf-king) is a malevolent sprite who preys upon children and lures them into his domain of death. Late one night a man is riding his horse through the forest (a very Romantic *locus*), his young son sitting behind him and clasping his neck. The boy calls to his father that he sees the Erlking, but the father dismisses his son with naturalistic explanations for what the boy sees: a streak of mist, the wind sighing through dead leaves, old willows shimmering so gray. The Erlking's cajoling eventually turns into nastiness; the boy becomes more insistent; finally, the father believes him and rides like the wind to the *Hof* (the courtyard of an inn). Alas, his son is already dead when they arrive.

How does Schubert interpret this poem in music? There are four characters—narrator, father, boy, and Erlking—but only one singer. Schubert delineates them through vocal range: The narrator sings mostly in medium range, the father in low range, and the boy in high range. The Erlking also sings in medium range, but in the major mode, whereas the three other roles sing in minor mode. The piano accompaniment also narrates; the pianist's right hand plays repeated octave triplets, while the left hand plays triplets in a sweeping, wave-like motion. Toward the end of *Erlkönig* the tempo reaches a furious pace, but as the father rides into the inn's courtyard, the tempo slows down to mimic the horse's slowing down to a walk and then stopping. The narrator bluntly sings: "In his arms the child was dead." This *Lied*, with its macabre ending, was fortunately not the only type of song that Schubert composed; he also had a gift for melody and even comedy. These attributes can be heard, for example, in *Ständchen* (*Serenade*) and in *Die Forelle* (*The Trout*). Schubert's famous *Ave Maria*, by the way, was originally a *Lied*—*Ellens dritter Gesang*—which was later adapted to Latin. Schubert set a German translation of a song from Sir Walter Scott's narrative poem *The Lady of the Lake*. Ellen, the protagonist, is indeed singing to the Blessed Virgin—including the refrain *Ave Maria*—but she is not singing the *Hail Mary* prayer.

Other great composers of *Lieder* included brother and sister Felix and Fanny Mendelssohn, Johannes Brahms, Gustav Mahler, Richard Strauss, and the Schumanns—Robert and his wife, Clara. Many of the above characteristics can be found in the songs of Robert Schumann, who composed four hundred-plus *Lieder*. A great number of them date from 1840, the year of his marriage to Clara Wieck, the daughter of his piano teacher. Clara, for her part, responded with her own *Lieder*, such as the exquisite *Liebst du um Schönheit*. In Robert's *Liederkreis* (which means "song cycle"), we encounter a female malevolent sprite—the Lorelei—in his song *Waldesgespräch*. Also, there is limpid lyricism in *Intermezzo*, another

Lied from the Op. 39 *Liederkreis*, settings of lyric poetry by Joseph von Eichendorff.

Robert was also a pioneer of the character piece, a new Romantic genre of piano music. This short piece usually had a free, innovative form—which accorded well with Romantics' disinclination to use strict classical forms—and some descriptive, or programmatic, elements. *Carnaval* is a set of twenty-one character pieces Robert composed from 1834 to 1835; they are musically linked by the use of three sets of a cryptic four-note melodic motive based on letters from Schumann's name. *Carnaval* depicts the guests at a masked ball held during carnival season, prior to Lent. Some guests are real people, like *Chiarina* (Clara) and *Chopin*, but some are fictitious characters—and even alter egos—of Robert, for example, Eusebius (his reflective side) and Florestan (his fiery and impetuous side). Also depicted are the violin virtuoso Paganini and several characters from *commedia dell'arte*—Pierrot, Harlequin, Colombina, and Pantalone.

Frédéric (Fryderyk) Chopin (1810–1849), one of the guests depicted in *Carnaval*, first become known to Robert Schumann in 1831, as Robert revealed in an article he wrote for a German music journal. Robert depicted a conversation among some imaginary members of the equally imaginary *League of David* (*Davidsbündler*), two of whom we met in *Carnaval*. Eusebius was the gentle dreamer, Florestan the impulsive, and Master Raro, the wise old scholar. The *League of David* was in constant battle against the Philistines, Robert's name for musicians and audiences whose tastes tended toward the trite, banal, and unartistic commercial music of the day.

In Schumann's article, these three characters comment on the "genius" evident in Chopin's early Opus 2 piano Variations on "Là ci darem la mano," the Act II duet from Mozart's opera *Don Giovanni*, as Eusebius plays from the previously unknown score. In 1831 Chopin (1810–1849) was only about twenty-one, and he would become much more well known for new Romantic piano genres such as nocturne, prelude, concert etude, ballade, scherzo, and dances from his native Poland, such as mazurka and polonaise. One Romantic piano genre inextricably linked to Chopin is the nocturne. He did not invent it but he suffused it with innovations. The "inventor" of the nocturne was the Irish pianist and composer John Field (1782–1837). Liszt paid tribute to Field's nocturnes and revealed the Romantic attitude toward music composition when he described Field's nocturnes as

> the first attempts ... to infuse the piano with feelings and dreams and to free piano music from the constraints imposed until then by regular and "official" form on compositions of all kinds. Before him they all had of necessity to be cast as sonatas or rondos or some such. Field, contrariwise, introduced a genre that belonged to none of these existing categories, in which feeling and melody reigned supreme, and which moved freely, without the fetters and constraints of any preconceived form.[2]

Field's nocturnes are lovely, but it is Chopin's nocturnes that have achieved musical immortality. Chopin's Nocturne in D-flat, Opus 27, No. 2, displays characteristics that emulate Field, but also traits that show Chopin's originality and enrichment of the genre. To continue Liszt's description of Field—here applied to Chopin—the long-lined righthand melody (reminiscent of a *bel canto* opera aria by Bellini) is "festooned ... with uninterrupted arabesques and garlands. . . . The melodies never disappeared beneath the ornaments, whose

2   Lina Ramann, ed. *Gesammelte Schriften von Franz Liszt*, IV (Leipzig, 1882), trans. Richard Taruskin, quoted in Piero Weiss and Richard Taruskin, eds., *Music in the Western World: A History in Documents*, 2nd ed. (Belmont, CA: Schirmer Cengage Learning, 2005), 313.

languorous billows and exquisitely graceful tracery veiled them but never covered them up."[3] The left hand spreads out over the lower notes of the piano in widely spaced broken chords, the slow 6/8 meter imparting "a language as coaxing as a tearful look, as lulling as the even back-and forth of a rocking boat or a swinging hammock, whose languorously easeful movements persuade us that we hear the sweetest of breezes whispering all around us."[4] The key of D-flat major has five flats, and this imparts an extra-warm timbre. This nocturne has two stanzas, with the second stanza going to a new key area, beginning in B-flat minor but traversing various keys until the first stanza returns in the home key of D-flat. Each stanza is repeated and varied in ever more ornate versions, spanning qualities from languid to ecstatic. These were qualities that were well appreciated by Romantics.

Chopin became a fixture in French society, including cohabitation with the novelist George Sand (Aurore Dudevant). Chopin had lapsed from his Catholic faith, but James Huneker, in his biography of Chopin, recalls the eyewitness account by Father Alexander Jelowicki of the composer's deathbed reconversion to his Catholic faith. Father Jelowicki, a long-time friend, was able to cooperate with grace and bring the last rites to Chopin, who ultimately received the grace to accept them.[5]

---

3   Ibid., 312.
4   Ibid.
5   James Huneker, *Chopin, the Man and His Music* (Garden City, NY: Dover Publications, 1966), 72–80.

19

Romantic Italian Opera

In an 1823 letter to his friend Vincent Novello, Anglo-Italian organist and music publisher, Leigh Hunt described the contemporary musical scene in Italy and the composer who dominated it.

> You ask me to tell you a world of things about Italian composers, singers, etc. Alas! my dear N. I may truly say to you that, for music, you must "look at home"—at least, as far as my own experience goes. But I will tell you one thing which, albeit you are of Italian origin, will mortify you to hear, namely, that Mozart is nothing in Italy, and Rossini everything. Nobody ever says anything of Mozart since "Figaro" (tell it not in Gothland!) *was hissed at Florence.* His name appears to be suppressed by agreement, while Rossini is talked of, written of, copied, sung, hummed, whistled, and demi-semi-quavered from morning to night. If there is a portrait in a shop-window, it is Rossini's. If you hear a song in the street, it is Rossini's. If you go to a music-shop to have something copied—"An air of Rossini's?"[1]

Hunt—a writer, and friend of Shelley, Keats, and Byron—was writing from Italy, where he had witnessed the vogue for Rossini's operas.

---

1   Mary Cowden-Clarke, "Leigh Hunt," *Century Illustrated Monthly Magazine*, XXIII (March 1882), n.s. 1, 708–9, quoted in Piero Weiss and Richard Taruskin, eds., *Music in the Western World: A History in Documents*, 2nd ed. (Belmont, CA: Schirmer Cengage Learning, 2005), 286.

After initial successes at a small Venetian theatre, Gio-achino Rossini (1792–1868) composed operas for several other theatres and then, in 1815, landed a contract in Naples as music director for the royal theatres. The seven years Rossini spent there provided him with stability that favored his development as a composer. While there he composed mainly serious operas like *Otello*, *Mosè in Egitto*, and *La donna del lago*.

Also in Naples Rossini composed works for other opera houses, including two of his most famous comic operas, *The Barber of Seville* and *La Cenerentola*. The libretto of *The Barber* was based on the first play of Beaumarchais' trilogy, which also includes *The Marriage of Figaro*. Rossini composed the music in three weeks, and *The Barber* (1816) remains his most famous opera. The story tells of how Count Almaviva, assisted by his valet Figaro, outwits Dr. Bartolo and elopes with his ward Rosina. *La Cenerentola* (1817) is a retelling of "Cinder-ella," complete with hilarious ugly stepsisters and stepmother, but has some details different from the story familiar to Amer-icans. Both of these comic masterpieces illustrate the musical hallmarks that made Rossini so successful.

Audiences loved the build-up of action and musical dynamics in Rossini's operas, especially in finales, which usu-ally featured a huge *crescendo* as the music became livelier and noisier with the addition of more instruments to the orches-tra. Also popular in Rossini's comic operas were solo sections in *parlante* style, singing in a speechlike manner above an orchestral melody. The Gilbert and Sullivan "patter song" is a descendant of this (think, "I am the very model of a modern major-general").

In 1823 his serious opera *Semiramide* failed at its Venice premiere and Rossini moved to Paris. There he composed two French operas—*Le Comte Ory* (1828), an *opéra comique*, and a grand opera, *Guillaume Tell* (1829). By 1823, when Leigh Hunt wrote his letter to Novello, Rossini had almost finished his operatic career. Inexplicably, Rossini retired from composing operas in 1829, when he was in his late thirties. Rossini did not stop composing altogether, and in his remaining years he composed songs, a setting of *Stabat Mater* (1842), and his *Petite Messe solennelle* (1863), a Mass for small choir, soloists, two pianos, and harmonium. Although Rossini was successful with both serious and comic opera, it was the comic for which he was most loved. *The Barber of Seville* (*Il barbiere in Siviglia*), *The Italian Girl in Algiers* (*L'Italian in Algeri*), and *Cinderella* (*La Cenerentola*) are staples in the world's opera houses to this day, and Rossini's sparkling music still delights audiences.

In nineteenth-century Italy opera was everything; it was a huge commercial venture in which the composer was not an object of worship but a servant of the impresario, the star singers, and the ticket-buying audience. The eighteenth-century traditions of *opera seria* and *opera buffa* carried on into the nineteenth, although *opera seria* assimilated certain aspects of *opera buffa*; this mixed genre was named *opera semiseria*.

Rossini was not the only composer with a gift for melody; it seems to have been a particularly Italian trait. Nineteenth-century Italian opera is often associated with the term *bel canto*, which literally means "beautiful song," a style of lyrical, smooth singing with uniformly beautiful tone from lowest to highest notes of a singer's range. Pure vowels, native to the Italian language, are all-important, as are good taste and the ability to improvise vocal embellishments. The music of Rossini and his successors, Donizetti and Bellini, epitomizes the *bel canto* style.

Gaetano Donizetti (1797–1848) was only a few years younger than Rossini, though he died before Rossini, and he is remembered equally for his serious and his comic operas, which total about seventy. Donizetti's best-known comic operas include *L'elisir d'amore* (*The Elixir of Love*, 1832), *Don*

Pasquale (1843), and *La fille du régiment* (*The Daughter of the Regiment*, 1840), which he composed for Paris.

Donizetti moved to Naples at about the time Rossini was leaving there. Until 1830 Donizetti was lauded for comic opera, but in that year his serious opera *Anna Bolena* premiered successfully; subsequently his serious operas began to gain renown.

In the early Romantic era there was among writers and musicians in many countries a keen interest in all things English. In music this can be seen in a series of operas centering on English history; Rossini had already composed his own Tudor opera, *Elisabetta Regina d'Inghilterra*, in 1815. Donizetti's first Tudor opera was *Elisabetta al castello di Kenilworth* (1829), followed by *Anna Bolena, Maria Stuarda* (1835), and *Roberto Devereux* (1837), which chronicles the relationship between Elizabeth I and the Earl of Essex. The novels and poetry of Sir Walter Scott provided another popular source of opera librettos. Rossini responded with *La donna del lago* (*The Lady of the Lake*, 1819) and from Donizetti's pen came *Lucia di Lammermoor* (1835), an adaptation of Scott's *The Bride of Lammermoor* (1819).

Vincenzo Bellini (1801–1835) was born last and died young, before both Rossini and Donizetti. He composed only nine operas but achieved great fame for his elegant recitatives and archetypal *bel canto* arias with supple, flowing lines building up to affecting climaxes. One of Bellini's most acclaimed operas is *I puritani* (1835), English-themed but set after the Tudor era. It involves love and conflict during the English Civil War (1642–1649). Likewise English-themed, but set much earlier, is *Norma*, which involves the love between Norma, a Druid priestess, and Pollione, an officer of the occupying Roman army. *Casta diva* is the most celebrated aria from *Norma* and illustrates superbly Bellini's beautiful, long-breathed, and ornate melodies.

The summit of Romantic Italian opera is Giuseppe Verdi (1813–1901), who continued the melodic tradition of his predecessors but added more depth and drama. Verdi built on their style and attained even more flexibility of harmony and phrase structure, which allowed him to express emotions more strongly. This new, more dramatic vocal writing demanded a type of singing that challenged the *bel canto* tradition.

Verdi's career did not start until 1836, after Rossini's retirement and Bellini's death. He drew his librettos from contemporary authors such as Victor Hugo and Alexandre Dumas, Jr., but he also used venerable authors like Shakespeare and Tasso. Verdi had good instincts about what would work well on stage and he collaborated closely with his librettists. His mix of intense emotional circumstances, fast-paced action, and violence were attractive to Italian audiences.

Political liberty was a significant theme in several of Verdi's operas because of his sympathy for the *Risorgimento*. Verdi was from northern Italy, which was dominated by Austria. Italy at this time was not a single nation but a cluster of various "states." The *Risorgimento* was founded to unify these states into one state, the Kingdom of Italy. The movement was complex, with one facet of the *Risorgimento* being its ties to Freemasonry through the Italian secret society called the *Carboneria*; thus, there was an anti-Catholic element to it. "Va, pensiero," Verdi's famous chorus of Hebrew slaves, from his early opera *Nabucco* (1842), is the most famous of his opera choruses that alluded to the ideals of the *Risorgimento*.

One of the jewels of Verdi's early period, which also includes *Rigoletto* and *Il trovatore*, was *La traviata* (1853). *La traviata* is based on the play *La Dame aux camélias*, by Alexandre Dumas, Jr., which in turn was based on his novel inspired by Abbé Prévost's novel *Manon Lescaut* (1731) and by a real woman, Alphonsine Duplessis, who died in Paris in 1847, at age twenty-three. Verdi's operatic adaptation premiered in Venice on March 6, 1853. *La traviata* is remarkable for its plot, which is set not in the historic past but in Verdi's own time. The story is of thwarted love, as Violetta, the heroine, is a courtesan who is unacceptable to the family of Alfredo, her true love. Although Alfredo's father eventually accepts Violetta, it is too late. She dies of tuberculosis. Musical styles alternate between the frivolity of Violetta's social milieu and the sincerity of her developing integrity. Verdi populates the opera with various forms of the waltz, very much background music of that day, with both Violetta and Alfredo having exquisite music in waltz tempo to sing. After *Aïda* (1871), Verdi retired from composing, except for his Requiem (1874), until he was persuaded by his librettist Arrigo Boïto to adapt Shakespeare's *Othello* as an opera. This late masterpiece premiered, to great acclaim, in 1887. Verdi was not done yet, however, for he still had one masterpiece to compose. Again, it was Boïto who encouraged Verdi, and who adapted the libretto of *Falstaff* from *The Merry Wives of Windsor* and *Henry V*, Parts I and II. *Falstaff* premiered in 1893; after an operatic career focused on serious operas, Verdi's swan song was an effervescent comedy.

Verdi's "successor," Giacomo Puccini (1858–1924), was born into a dynasty of musicians. Beginning his creative life as a composer in the tradition of Verdi, around 1890 he adopted *verismo*, a new style developed by Pietro Mascagni (1863–1945). The year 1890 was the year that Mascagni's *Cavalleria rusticana* (*Rustic Chivalry*) premiered and launched the *verismo* movement. The Italian word *verismo* means "realism," and operas of Mascagni, Puccini, and Leoncavallo depicted real life, with raw emotion and violence such as had never been seen before in the theatre. For Puccini *verismo* was typified in *Tosca* (1900) and in his one-act opera *Il Tabarro* (1918). *Tosca* is set in Rome and is based on history, at the moment when Rome's domination by the Kingdom of Naples is endangered by Napoleon's imminent takeover of Italy. The opera includes torture (offstage), ruthless political machinations by the police chief Scarpia, and the onstage murder of Scarpia by Floria Tosca, the opera singer who is trying to save her lover, Mario Cavaradossi, from political execution. In the final scene, at Rome's Castel Sant'Angelo, Tosca leaps off the castle's parapet to her death as soldiers come to seize her after they execute Mario.

Tosca also illustrates some of Puccini's musical style traits. The opera includes at least four instances of what could be called arias, extended melodic sections that could stand alone outside the opera, yet Puccini's operas are routinely through-composed, meaning that each scene flows musically and smoothly into the next, with no divisions into self-contained, closed, numbers. Verdi had already begun this process in *Otello* and *Falstaff*. Unlike most Italian composers, Puccini incorporated elements of French and German orchestral color, including Wagnerian chromatic harmony. He also used motives throughout *Tosca* to distinguish characters and emotions, somewhat like Wagner's leitmotifs; Scarpia, for instance, is identified by a powerful chord progression.

Puccini's *Tosca*, along with *La bohème* and *Madama Butterfly*, are among the top ten operas performed worldwide. Puccini's continuing influence is evident in the musicals *Miss Saigon*, adapted from *Madama Butterfly*, and *Rent*, adapted from *La Bohème*.

20

Liszt and Wagner

Chopin, Robert Schumann, Wagner, and Verdi are some Romantic composers whose lives intersected with Franz Liszt's, as all were born between 1810 and 1813. Of these—all of whom lived dramatic lives—none had a life of more extreme contrasts than Liszt. There is the portrait of Liszt as virtuoso pianist with long, flowing hair. This Franz Liszt played piano works full of scales and bombastic chords, and he was worshipped as an idol by hordes of adoring female fans. There is another Franz Liszt, though. This Liszt was introspective, contemplative, pious, and in his later years would compose music of extremely sparse textures using a harmonic palette that foreshadowed twentieth-century music. This Liszt also later moved to Rome and was ordained to the minor orders, stopping short of the subdiaconate, diaconate, and the priesthood.

Which is the real Liszt? Many of his contemporaries, as well as later biographers, saw Liszt's taking up of holy orders as hypocritical, but if one examines Liszt's entire life, it may be possible to reconcile this seeming disparity and to trace the progress of a soul. Liszt's father, Adam, who added the "z" to his surname "List," had spent almost two years in the Franciscan order.[1] As the "priest" of his "domestic church," Adam saw to it that Franz was taught the faith, the lives of the saints, and the Church's liturgical life. Thus, from an early age and

---

1 Franz would later become a Franciscan tertiary.

throughout most of his life, Franz Liszt had a strong faith and a penchant for the contemplative life, all the more amazing when one considers the periods of his life as traveling virtuoso pianist, conductor, and composer.

Besides the Church, a second influence that stands out among the experiences of Liszt's early life was gypsy music, which he often heard played by Romany virtuoso fiddlers. It was the spontaneous and improvisatory nature of gypsy music that appealed so much to Franz. This can account, partially, for his impulse to improvise, which he did with astounding inventiveness, and it can also account, perhaps, for Liszt's colorful and often daring harmonies. Even as a young boy Franz revealed a predilection for unusual harmonies, and over the years he progressed so far harmonically that his late piano music—for example, *Nuages gris*—prefigures the unconventional harmonic language of Claude Debussy or even the atonality of Arnold Schoenberg. These two early formative experiences can provide clues to the mystery of his music and of his being.

Liszt's father, a gifted amateur cellist, noticed his son's remarkable talent, but after a few years of piano lessons Adam decided to relocate to Vienna so that eleven-year-old Franz could study with Carl Czerny, Beethoven's former student and now a master pedagogue. However, after eighteen months of lessons, poverty and an eye to his son's career impelled Adam to move on to Paris. The trip from Vienna to Paris was the beginning of Franz's career as a touring virtuoso, as Adam had set up concerts in several cities *en route*. At some point during these earliest years of touring, Franz felt a desire to become a priest, but his father told him that art, not the Church, was his vocation.

When Franz was sixteen his father died unexpectedly; now he had to manage his own life and also look after his mother. All of this produced a crisis in the teenager's life; he retreated from touring and began to live an undisciplined and aimless life. After two years Franz emerged from this period of depression. He again began to practice, perform, and compose, and he embarked upon the pursuit of knowledge and worldly pleasures, for which he was to become known almost as much as for his astounding pianistic powers.

From the age of seventeen Liszt had several love affairs, but two women figure most prominently in his life. When he was twenty-one Franz met Countess Marie d'Agoult. This relationship lasted until 1844 and produced three children: Blandine, Cosima (later married to Richard Wagner), and Daniel. The couple traveled much, but they spent some years in Switzerland, which inspired Liszt to compose piano pieces describing scenes of great natural beauty in that country. Eventually they were published as Volume I of Liszt's *Années de pèlerinage* (*Years of Pilgrimage*).

In 1839 Liszt resumed his concert tours and until 1847 enjoyed his greatest period of fame. While on tour in 1847—at a concert in Kiev—Liszt met his second love, Princess Carolyne von Sayn-Wittgenstein. Tired of touring, Liszt accepted a position as music director at the ducal court of Weimar. Carolyne joined Franz, who stayed at Weimar thirteen years, during which he developed as a composer of such orchestral masterworks as *Tasso*, one of twelve symphonic poems, and the *Dante* and *Faust* symphonies. Liszt and the princess, who was separated from her husband, always intended to marry, but over the years, every attempt to obtain an annulment of her marriage ended in failure, thanks to the machinations of her powerful in-laws, who did not want to lose her vast wealth. The final straw came in Rome, in 1862, after Carolyne had appealed to Pope Pius IX; the annulment was granted but then revoked twelve hours before the couple's wedding. Liszt and Carolyne spent their remaining years in separate apartments in Rome, still soul mates to the end.

Liszt's prodigious pianism owed much to the inspiration of the Italian violinist Niccolò Paganini (1782–1840). Paganini, through his own compositions and his virtuoso playing, had developed a reputation for doing things on the violin that had never been done before. After hearing Paganini perform in April 1832, Liszt decided that he would do for the piano what Paganini had done for the violin. Liszt took Paganini's *24 Caprices*, Opus 1, for solo violin, as his starting point and composed his own études displaying a pianistic style that was fiendishly difficult.

Other innovations of Liszt include the solo piano recital and the symphonic poem. Prior to Liszt a pianist would share a recital with other artists, but Liszt introduced the solo recital. Further, in order to achieve better acoustics Liszt inaugurated the now standard placement of the piano—sideways, with the opened lid tilted out toward the audience and the pianist in profile.

The symphonic poem departed from the symphony—normally a work of four movements—in that it has only one movement. Liszt, with his strong inclination toward literature and other arts, determined that the symphonic poem should be programmatic. He desired to break free from the strictures of Classical forms and thought that music needed to express extra-musical ideas or objects in a freer and more imaginative way. This he did through his concept of thematic transformation, in which a melodic theme is used many times in a work but modified, or transformed, to represent different ideas, as in his symphonic poem *Les Préludes*.

Liszt's flamboyant lifestyle sometimes obscured his true musical contributions, just as it obscured his deep Catholic faith. May future generations take time to study the life and music of this complex and magnanimous genius.

In 1870 Richard Wagner married Cosima Liszt von Bülow, the daughter of Franz Liszt. At the time of their marriage Wagner was finishing *Siegfried*, the third of four music dramas—*Das Rheingold, Die Walküre, Siegfried*, and *Götterdämmerung*—which comprise *Der Ring des Nibelungen* (*The Ring of the Nibelung*), finally premiering in August of 1876.

Wagner's ideal of music drama was a "united work of art" (*Gesamtkunstwerk*) in which all elements—music, poetry, acting, dance, painting, architecture, and sculpture—work together seamlessly. Wagner was able to do this because he controlled every element of production. He composed both music and libretto and also closely oversaw scenic and lighting design. Wagner even went so far as to have a special theatre designed that would provide the optimum environment for the *Ring*. This was the *Festspielhaus* at Bayreuth, underwritten by King Ludwig II of Bavaria.

Through his use of short melodic motives known as leitmotifs ("leading motives")—linked to a character, emotion, idea, or object—Wagner was able to influence and affect the emotions of his audience. The orchestra does the main work of playing these leitmotifs as a kind of subtext beneath the sung poetry of the music drama. One masterful example where several leitmotifs are presented together is at the end of *Die Walküre* (*The Valkyrie*), after Wotan has consigned his daughter Brünnhilde to sleep on a rock, forever surrounded by magic fire unless she can be rescued by a hero who knows no fear. The "magic fire," kindled by the god Loge, has a leitmotif of sparkling arpeggiated figures, while the fanfare-like "Siegfried" motive blares out from the brass, thus revealing the identity of the hero who is to come. Also heard are leitmotifs associated with "magic sleep," "slumber," and "fate." All are blended into a magnificent finale that moves the listener to feelings of awe and enchantment. As Wagner developed his ideas and put them into use in his music dramas, his use of leitmotifs evolved. In *Tristan und Isolde* (1865) and

Parsifal (1882) there are fewer motifs but Wagner uses them more flexibly.

As with the *Ring* cycle, Wagner's *Parsifal*—his final music drama—presents a synthesis of sources, resulting in his unique "take" on a medieval tale stemming from the Arthurian legends. But whereas the *Ring* is concerned with pre-Christian mythology, *Parsifal*—particularly in Wagner's adaptation—is fraught with patently Christian symbolism. At the same time, however, it does not have an exact correlation with orthodox Christian theology. This would produce, in its reception history, a plethora of opinions on the message of *Parsifal*.

In the Arthurian legends, Parsifal (Percival) is associated with his quest for the Holy Grail, but in Wagner's opera, the hero encounters the Grail (as a physical object) without searching for it. To make a long story short, here is a very condensed summary of Wagner's *Parsifal*. Parsifal's years of wandering have taught him much and caused him to mature into the hero and healer who was predicted to come to the rescue of Amfortas, the wounded king of the Grail Knights. Parsifal's first moment of compunction and compassion comes in Act I, when he shoots down a swan. In the Act II scene with Kundry, Parsifal gains in compassion and sympathy. He is spiritually able to assume the wound of Amfortas and to repel, and thus redeem, Kundry. This imbues Parsifal with Christ-like qualities, and indeed, he turns out to be the long-awaited redeemer of Amfortas and the knights, as well as of Kundry. Did Wagner intend Parsifal to be seen as Christ, or as a type of Christ? The sacred rite of the Grail Knights superficially resembles the Liturgy of the Eucharist, but it by no means replicates the Mass. What was Wagner's intention?

Many have speculated about *Parsifal*'s meaning. Since 1854 Wagner had been an admirer of Schopenhauer's philosophy, a philosophy that—in common with Buddhism—emphasized compassion and renunciation of the will. It is popular among writers of today to claim that Wagner was promoting Schopenhauerian and Buddhist ideas. Others see Wagner's "faith" as philosophical, not religious. However, when he became aware of *Parsifal*, the apostate former Lutheran seminarian Nietzsche broke off his friendship with Wagner and railed against the hated Christianity that he perceived in the opera. He seems to have seen something that eluded the many who had come to substitute art for religion.

Wagner, a nominal Lutheran, was a native of Saxony, that most Protestant part of Germany. His earlier writings reveal a man who is dismissive of Christianity, and particularly of Catholicism; for example, he accused Christianity of destroying the art of drama, and his personal life was not an example of Christian virtue. Yet, as he neared the end of his life, he wrote to his patron, King Ludwig II of Bavaria: "It seems to me as if the making of this work [*Parsifal*] has been entrusted to me in order to uphold to the world its own most profound mystery, the truth of the Christian faith; indeed, even to rekindle this faith."[2]

---

2   O. Strobel, ed. *König Ludwig II und Richard Wagner Briefwechsel,* vol. 3 (Karlsruhe, 1936–1939), 21–22, quoted in Lucy Beckett, *Richard Wagner: Parsifal* (Cambridge: Cambridge University Press, 1981), 138.

21

Central European Romantics
and Post-Romantics

A cluster of Central European composers, all of whom are either late or post-Romantic, are the focus of this chapter. If Anton Bruckner (1824–1896) had died at thirty-five, when Mozart did, his music would be unknown today, yet Bruckner is now acknowledged as one of the greatest symphonic composers of the nineteenth century. His symphonies are huge episodic constructions, described as "cathedrals" by some; listeners tend either to turn away in impatience or to become fans. What is the secret behind this humble, self-effacing man who composed such masterful symphonies and sublime sacred music?

Anton's father was a schoolmaster, which put him in contact with Austria's rich musical culture because his job also included being organist at the local parish. Anton's first exposure to music was in church, where he would sit next to his father on the organ bench or be with his mother when the choir sang at High Mass. At ten, Anton was already a skilled organist, and at eleven he began to study harmony. After his father's death, in 1837, Anton's mother enrolled him in choir school at the nearby Augustinian priory of Saint Florian. For three years Anton continued his education and grew in musical prowess, especially in organ improvisation. Despite this, when Anton's voice changed and he had to move on to an adult career, he took the safe route of enrolling in a teacher-training program at Linz, which enabled Anton to hear, for the first time, secular concert music by masters like Weber and Beethoven.

The young schoolmaster-organist endured jobs in two small towns before he returned in 1845 to Saint Florian as first assistant teacher. By 1851 Bruckner had become principal organist at Saint Florian; now he could become a full-time musician. Throughout his twenties Bruckner progressed in composition until a visiting organist encouraged him to take a correspondence course in counterpoint and harmony with Simeon Sechter, former teacher of Schubert.

At thirty, Bruckner broadened his horizons by becoming cathedral organist at Linz; here he stayed for thirteen years. After completing his course with Sechter—in which he impressed the examiners—the thirty-seven-year-old Bruckner decided to increase his knowledge of orchestration and symphonic form through study with cellist and conductor Otto Kitzler. It was thanks to him that Bruckner was exposed to Wagner's music, a seminal experience that occurred in 1862 when Kitzler produced the Linz premiere of *Tannhäuser*. It was a revelation to Bruckner that Wagner could compose such superlative music while nonetheless transgressing many rules of harmony and counterpoint that Sechter had taught. Now Bruckner had courage to reveal the music that had been inside him for so long; the revelation of his mature style came in 1864 with his Mass in D minor.

In 1868 Bruckner moved to Vienna, where he lived for the rest of his life and experienced much artistic growth while becoming the center of musical controversy. Many Viennese were not ready for Bruckner's originality. Vienna Philharmonic musicians railed against Bruckner's symphonies, considering them too bold or "unplayable," even though such a luminary as Liszt lauded Bruckner's Second Symphony.

Well-meaning friends talked the insecure Bruckner into shortening and making alterations to his symphonies, to make them more acceptable to public taste.

By 1884, however, when the Seventh Symphony premiered, Bruckner's coterie of supporters had expanded. This time his symphony was played without cuts by the Leipzig Gewandhaus Orchestra and was applauded for fifteen minutes. Now Bruckner had truly arrived, and he began to be recognized as a great composer outside of Austria, even as far away as America. Bruckner began his Ninth Symphony in 1889 and dedicated it to "the King of Kings, our Lord," but at his death in 1896, only the first three movements were completed.

Though Bruckner is known primarily as a symphonic composer, his sacred music deserves to be better known. Bruckner's Catholic faith shines forth in his liturgical music, from the sublime motets *Ave Maria* and *Os iusti* to his larger sacred choral works. Bruckner's Masses and his *Te Deum* are like vocal symphonies, or as some have commented, his symphonies are rather like "Masses without words."

Anton Bruckner was simple yet complex; he was a musical genius who emerged from the Austrian peasantry. Though personally insecure and always feeling the need for more study, this devout Catholic worked doggedly, confident that God was guiding him. Bruckner's originality, the vastness of his symphonic design, and the episodic character of his symphonies may well have their roots in his background as an improviser at the organ. Through his music Bruckner approached God with love and awe.

Unlike pious Catholics Bruckner and Dvořák, Johannes Brahms (1833–1897) was a Bible-reading Lutheran agnostic from northern Germany. Brahms excelled not only at orchestral music, but also at piano music, chamber music, and *Lieder*. Among his many wonderful songs are *Die Mainacht* and

Sonntag, and his piano *Intermezzi*, for instance, are like songs without words. Settling permanently in Vienna around 1862, Brahms was championed by music critic Eduard Hanslick as the standard bearer for "absolute music," that is, music with no story to tell outside of itself, unlike program music. Absolute genres included the symphony, which follows a standard form; this kind of music was rejected by Liszt and other members of the "New German School," who felt fettered by classic forms.

The specter of Beethoven was a major factor in Brahms's twenty-year procrastination in finishing his First Symphony. He famously said: "You don't know what it feels like to have a giant like Beethoven dogging your footsteps!" Brahms began his First Symphony in the early 1860s but did not finish until 1876. The influence of Beethoven's Symphony No. 5 was evident in its key—C minor—and in the triumphant finale in C major. After Brahms's First Symphony, his other three followed in relatively close succession (1877, 1883, 1885), and his future was secured as a major composer.

One of Brahms's immortal works is his German Requiem (*Ein deutsches Requiem*), which is not a liturgical work, like musical settings of the Catholic Requiem Mass. Brahms chose biblical passages that had meaning for him and were comforting in the face of the deaths of his mother and of Robert Schumann.

Brahms befriended and helped promote Antonin Dvořák, eight years his junior. Brahms had served as an adjudicator for the Vienna State Prize, awarded to Dvořák for three years in a row (1875–1877). Dvořák revered and emulated Brahms as a composer, and Brahms greatly admired the Czech composer's fresh and unaffected melodic gift. Of Brahms, the confirmed bachelor who referred to his German Requiem as a "Human" Requiem, Dvořák, the family man and faithful Catholic would say, "Such a man, such a fine soul—and he believes in nothing, he believes in nothing!"[1] Yet despite their differing temperaments and world-views, they remained good friends for the rest of their lives.

The tiny hamlet of Spillville, Iowa, has renown far beyond its size, for it played host to Dvořák during the summer of 1893. The house where Dvořák and his family stayed still stands; upstairs is the harmonium at which Dvořák composed during his sojourn in this Czech enclave.

In 1891 Dvořák was invited by Mrs. Jeannette Thurber, a wealthy New Yorker, to be director of the National Conservatory of Music she had started in 1885. Hiring a famous European composer as a means of promoting a truly American conservatory was a coup for her; the result for the history of American music was momentous.

Dvořák traveled to America with his wife, daughter, and oldest son in 1892, and began a three-year reign at the National Conservatory. After a year on the job, Dvořák was uncomfortable in his New York surroundings and homesick for Bohemia when an invitation came from Josef Jan Kovařík, his secretary, to spend a summer in Spillville. Kovařík was a native and his father was the local choirmaster and bandmaster. Dvořák readily accepted Josef Jan Kovařík's invitation, and happy with his decision, he wrote to a friend in Bohemia, "Everything is Czech. I shall be among my own folks and am looking forward to it very much."[2] During the spring, Dvořák finished a rough copy of his Symphony No. 9 ("From the New World") and then arranged to bring his other four children, with their aunt, to America. Reunited, the family departed on June 3, 1893, for Iowa, with Kovařík as guide. Upon arrival, Dvořák arose early the next morning and took a walk along the local Turkey River. The composer returned in

---

1   Otakar Sourek, *Antonín Dvořák: Letters and Reminiscences*, trans. Roberta Finlayson Samsour (Prague: Artia, 1954), 192.
2   Ibid., 157.

time to join his family for Mass at Saint Wenceslaus Church, but he crept upstairs to the organ loft. Parishioners at Low Mass were startled when Dvořák began to play the Czech hymn *Boze, pred tvou velobnosti* (*God, Before Thy Majesty*) and his family began to sing. Over time, however, the parishioners grew to enjoy the daily singing.

It did not take Dvořák long to compose new music inspired by Spillville; on June 10 he finished the sketch for his "American" Quartet, in F major, Opus 96. This string quartet, full of beauty and exuberance, includes a melodic motive in the *Scherzo* movement that some associate with the song of the scarlet tanager, a bird Dvořák heard for the first time in Spillville. In late June and early July Dvořák composed his string quintet in E-flat major, Opus 97, also known as the "American." There is much divergence of opinion over whether Dvořák incorporated melodic ideas from American Indian music that he might have heard in Spillville at a traveling "medicine show" that featured American Indian dances and music. Kovařík is said to have notated one of the Indian melodies that they heard, which Dvořák later used in the quintet.

In New York Dvořák had already been introduced to African American music through Harry T. Burleigh, a singer and composer who was a student at the National Conservatory. The *New York Herald* of May 21, 1893 reported on Dvořák's solution for an "American" music.

I am now satisfied that the future music of this country must be founded upon what are called the negro melodies ... [Negro melodies] are the folk songs of America and your composers must turn to them.... I did not come to America to interpret Beethoven or Wagner for the public.... I came to discover what young Americans had in them and to help them to express it.

Just as Dvořák had incorporated Bohemian dances and folk melodies into his own music (e.g., *Slavonic Dances*, Op. 46), so he saw America's indigenous music as inspiration for her composers. He was not discouraging Americans from using European musical forms and genres but he saw African American and American Indian music as appropriate starting points for a national music tradition. Later generations would thank Dvořák for this encouragement.

Gustav Mahler (1860–1911) is generally regarded as a post-Romantic composer, an icon of German Romanticism. He first gained success after the premiere of his Symphony No. 2, in 1895. Following Beethoven's precedent in his Ninth Symphony, Mahler scored the fourth and fifth movements of *his* symphony for chorus with soprano and alto soloists. It is these movements from which this symphony gets its nickname, "Resurrection," because of the sung lyrics. For the fourth movement, an alto solo, Mahler set *Urlicht* (*Ancient Light*), a poem evincing the soul's longing for God, from *Des Knaben Wunderhorn*, an 1805 collection of folk poems. For the fifth movement, the composer took only the first two stanzas of Klopstock's hymn *Die Auferstehung* (*The Resurrection*), which is about the resurrection of the body. Tellingly, in stanzas 1–2 Mahler omitted the word "Halleluia." The subsequent stanzas, not included by Mahler, make clear that *Auferstehung* refers to the Christian doctrine of the resurrection of the body, but stanzas 1–2, as used by Mahler, are not so explicit. Mahler added another twenty lines of ecstatic poetry that ignore God's final judgment and depict His acceptance of and love for the soul, thus departing from Christian teaching on the Day of Judgment. The beautiful, sublime, ecstatic ending of the "Resurrection" Symphony represents Mahler's personal vision of eternal life with God.

22

The Russians: Nineteenth Century

Nationalism was a major influence in nineteenth-century Europe. Prior to this, social and political philosophies had been supranational. The Roman Empire, and then the Holy Roman Empire, provided models of society and governance. Medieval culture was marked by a unified, Catholic outlook. The Renaissance culture of the Christian humanists, and all neo-classical cultures, looked to the civilizations of ancient Greece and Rome for inspiration.

Stirrings of nationalism began to be felt around the middle of the eighteenth century in some parts of Europe. Philosophical and literary currents that contributed to this included Rousseau's ideas of popular sovereignty and *volonté nationale* (national will). Collections of folk poetry by Thomas Percy and Johann Gottfried von Herder touched nationalistic sensibilities in Britain and in German-speaking lands. Also, various revolutionary struggles—for example, the American Revolution and the French Revolution—stimulated the growth of national pride. Artistic, literary, and musical movements affirming national identities began to appear. Interest in "peripheral" languages, such as Czech, Polish, and Russian, began to be used for literary works. In music, too, the phenomenon of nationalism became evident in a new enthusiasm for the special musical idioms that were thought to characterize a people, for example, the waltz in Vienna, the mazurka in Poland, the furiant in Bohemia, and others.

Russia will be the focus of our look at musical nationalism. Ever since Czar Peter I, "the Great" (r. 1682–1725) had
begun the Westernization of Russia; more elements of Western European culture were introduced to the vast, medieval,
and mostly rural landmass that was Imperial Russia. It was
during this period that Russia first became a great European
power. Peter established Saint Petersburg—named after his
patron saint—as his capital of Russia and sought to bring in
Western influences in ship building, government, military
organization, and fashion. Czarina Anna Ioannovna (r. 1730–
1740), Peter's niece, wished to have opera in her court, so in
1735 she imported Italian musicians. The Italians flourished
and continued during the reign of Catherine II, "the Great."
During her reign (1762–1796) she made an effort to import
the principles and practices of the European Enlightenment.
She encouraged the philosophy of the French Encyclopedists,
even to the point of inviting Denis Diderot to complete the
Encyclopédie in Saint Petersburg.

Russians became enamored of French culture, and both
French and Italian operas became a favorite entertainment at
court. Giovanni Paisiello's *The Barber of Seville* had its world
premiere in 1782 at the Imperial Court in Saint Petersburg.
Three other eighteenth-century Italian musical luminaries
who graced the Court during Catherine's reign were Giuseppe
Sarti, Domenico Cimarosa, and Baldassare Galuppi. Along
with the mostly serious Italian operas, comic operas also began
to be performed at the Imperial Court. This resulted in Russian musicians' seeking musical instruction from Italian composers, who were not interested in composing comic operas
themselves. Outside of Italian opera, the performance of
music from the late eighteenth to the mid-nineteenth century
was dominated by gifted amateur musicians of the aristocracy.

These noble dilettantes organized and performed in instrumental concerts. They also founded various organizations

like the St. Petersburg Philharmonic Society (1802), the Concert Society (1850), and the Imperial Russian Musical Society (IRMS). This last was founded in 1859 by Anton Rubinstein—an internationally known virtuoso pianist—and the Grand Duchess Elena Pavlovna, a patroness of the arts and a German-born aunt of the czar Alexander II. The IRMS became a catalyst for further developments in the empire's musical life, including Russia's first fully professional symphony orchestra. In 1862, Anton Rubinstein founded the Saint Petersburg Conservatory, the very first in Russia. His own musical education had included composition lessons in Berlin, so Rubinstein favored the German tradition of composition and music education. In 1860 the Mariinsky Theatre—for Russian opera—was opened, and in 1866 Anton's younger brother, pianist Nikolay Rubinstein, founded the Moscow Conservatory.

Nevertheless, in the 1850s and 1860s educated Russians were conflicted. On the one hand they saw that the answer to Russia's provincialism lay in openness to Western culture. On the other, they were interested in promoting a specifically Russian culture; thus, a musical controversy arose. Alexander Serov and Vladimir Stasov, two advocates of Russian nationalism, criticized the Rubinstein musical ventures for favoring Austro-German composers. Serov and Stasov were supporters of Russian music and the doctrine of "realism," founded principally by the literary critic Vissarion Belinsky.

All the most famous Russian composers of the Romantic era came of age during the reign of Czar Alexander II, who ascended the throne in 1855. In composition amateur musicians still held the field. Even Mikhail Glinka (1804–1857), Russia's first nationalistic composer, was not a professional musician, but a civil servant. Glinka, however, through his introduction of Russian folk melodies and folk-like melodies into his music—beginning with his operas *A Life for the Czar*

(1836) and *Ruslan and Ludmila* (1842)—pioneered a Russian nationalist style that was the inspiration for later Russian composers, particularly "The Five." The musical style of Glinka's operas was taken from Italian and French opera, but he added enough Russian elements—including an innovative style of recitative based on the Russian language—to establish himself as a founder of Russian classical music. Another founding composer was Alexander Dargomizhsky (1813–1869), whose experimentation with melodic declamation based on Russian speech declamation can be witnessed in his operas *Rusalka* (1856) and *The Stone Guest* (1872), its libretto based on Pushkin's retelling of the *Don Juan* story.

Following Glinka and Dargomiszhky, a new generation of composers made even more contributions to the development of a distinctive Russian musical style. In the early 1860s a group of five composers at odds with Western-dominated Russian music banded together and became known as the *moguchay kuchka* (mighty handful), or "The Five." They liked Western music but felt alienated from Saint Petersburg Conservatory and wanted to promote a Russian musical style.

All except Balakirev, the most professional of the Five, had had unconventional musical training. Mily Balakirev (1837–1910) made good use of folksong in his piano fantasia *Islamey* and his symphonic poem *Russia* (1887). He was the unacknowledged leader of the group and the teacher of Musorgsky. Alexander Borodin (1833–1887) was a chemist by profession and was originally attracted to the music of Felix Mendelssohn before Balakirev got him interested in Russian music. Even though Borodin did not often use actual folk songs in his music, he was a gifted composer of memorable melodies. In 1953 Robert Wright and George Forrest adapted several of them for the hit Broadway musical (and subsequent Hollywood film) *Kismet.* For instance, the *Polovtsian Dances* scene from Borodin's opera *Prince Igor* yielded the melodies for "Stranger in Paradise." The second movement of Borodin's String Quartet No. 2 furnished the melody for "Baubles, Bangles, and Beads," while "And This Is My Beloved" was borrowed from the third movement. César Cui (1835–1918), the least known of the Five, was an officer and engineer in the Imperial Russian Army. Although he was prolific as a composer, music was an avocation for him.

The central figure in the *Moguchay kuchka* was Modest Musorgsky (1839–1881), a clerk in the civil service. Musorgsky's major orchestral works include *A Night on Bald Mountain* (1867)[1] and *Pictures at an Exhibition* (1873), originally composed for piano but better known in Maurice Ravel's 1922 orchestral arrangement. *Pictures* is a suite of programmatic pieces, each piece representing a painting by Musorgsky's artist friend Viktor Hartmann, who had died at age thirty-nine. *Pictures'* subtitle was "In Remembrance of Viktor Hartmann." It was a retrospective exhibition of four hundred of Hartmann's paintings, out of which Musorgsky chose ten for the suite's movements. Several movements are linked by a *Promenade*, a musical interlude which depicts a viewer walking from painting to painting.

Musorgsky's operatic masterpiece *Boris Godunov* is a showpiece for the composer's "Russianness." The "Coronation Scene," while primarily featuring the chorus, also contains solo passages that illustrate Musorgsky's masterful approach to setting the Russian language, in which he was influenced by predecessors Glinka and Dargomiszhky. After acclamations of praise by the chorus of nobles and people (to a Russian folk melody), the newly crowned Czar Boris sings of his feelings of dread but then prays to God for divine assistance in being a good ruler. The people acclaim Czar Boris, and the scene ends with shouts of "Glory!"

---

1   It was used in Disney's *Fantasia.*

The fifth member of the *moguchay kuchka* was Nikolai Rimsky-Korsakov (1844–1908), who is celebrated for his symphonic suite *Scheherazade* but also for being the teacher of Igor Stravinsky.

One of the first students at Anton Rubinstein's Saint Petersburg Conservatory was Pyotr Ilyich Tchaikovsky (1840–1893), who at twenty-two was older than the typical new student. Although Tchaikovsky showed musical talent from an early age, his father wanted him to become a lawyer, so Pyotr was enrolled at the School of Jurisprudence. He finished legal studies in 1859 and then took a position as a clerk in the Ministry of Justice. This job, however, proved to be so unsatisfying and the call of music so tantalizing that Tchaikovsky quit his job in 1863, after he had already started composition study at the Conservatory. Upon his graduation in 1866, Tchaikovsky was engaged to teach harmony at the new Moscow Conservatory opened that year by Nikolay Rubinstein. The young professor was also active as a music critic, which helped augment his salary.

Tchaikovsky tried to reconcile his Western musical training at the Conservatory and his cosmopolitan family heritage (his mother was the descendant of a French immigrant) with native Russian elements. Some of Tchaikovsky's works that include Russian and Ukrainian elements are his Second Symphony ("Little Russian"), the finale from his Fourth Symphony, the *Marche Slav*, the *Andante cantabile* of his first string quartet, and *Dumka*, a piano piece.

Tchaikovsky adored Mozart's music and the music of other Western European composers, but he was also drawn to the emerging movement toward Russian nationalism. Thus, in 1868, when he met Balakirev—undeclared leader of the *moguchay kuchka*—Tchaikovsky was open to Balakirev's ideas and compositional advice. Balakirev gave Tchaikovsky the idea to compose a concert overture inspired by Shakespeare's

Romeo and Juliet, which would prove to be his earliest masterpiece. Disdainful of Western European abstract, absolute musical forms—which were the basis of Tchaikovsky's musical education—Balakirev urged Tchaikovsky to adopt a new approach to composition, what he called "dramatic scenarios." At first Tchaikovsky balked at this idea, which would identify *Romeo and Juliet* as program music, but then he relented and produced some scenes, though melded with sonata form.

The opening *Andante* acts as a slow introduction and features chordal and hymn-like music—suggesting Russian Orthodox polyphony—usually identified with Friar Laurence. It is first heard in the bassoons and the lower registers of the clarinets. It is then repeated in high registers of the woodwinds while the strings provide a *pizzicato* accompaniment. After a gradual buildup for 110 measures, an *Allegro giusto* "Exposition" starts and we hear the "Vendetta Theme." This loud, forceful, and sharply rhythmic first theme evokes the strife between the Capulets and Montagues, and the subsequent use of counterpoint suggests the swordfighting of the rival families. This theme is repeated *fortissimo* but then begins to soften when a sighing motive played by muted strings appears. This will eventually evolve into a second and gentler melody, the famous "Love Theme," which is played by the woodwinds. Obviously, this melody is associated with the all-consuming love between Romeo and Juliet; it is long-breathed, undulating, and unending.

As we know, however, the love of Romeo and Juliet ends tragically. Fragments of the Vendetta theme combined with the Hymn theme portend tragedy, except now the Hymn theme is faster, making it sound more like a march. Finally, we hear the Vendetta theme in its original key and then the Love theme. The coda—final ending—presents a slightly altered version of the Love theme, along with a new theme, and the work resolves gently in B major.

23

France from the *Belle époque* through World War I

In this chapter we shall survey France from 1871 until just after World War I, the era often styled the *Belle époque*. It began with the end of the Franco-Prussian War, in which France was defeated, and it saw a revival of French culture, including music and the restoration of Gregorian chant, begun in the 1850s at the Benedictine Abbey of Saint Peter of Solesmes. The three French composers who are this chapter's focus could be considered watershed composers in music history.

Gabriel Fauré (1845–1924) was born in Pamiers, in southwestern France. When he was about eight his musical talent began to be noticed and his father was advised to send Gabriel to a new music school in Paris. He arrived at the École Niedermeyer in October of 1854 to begin the school's rigorous curriculum, which consisted mainly of sacred music (plainsong, organ, Renaissance polyphony) and humanities. The students lived an ascetic life, but the musical instruction was superb; at the school Gabriel learned everything he would need to become a church musician.

In 1861 Niedermeyer—who was Gabriel's instructor in piano, plainsong, and composition—died. Providentially, his new piano teacher was Camille Saint-Saëns, who introduced Gabriel to music of contemporary composers like Schumann, Liszt, and Wagner. This, along with Saint-Saëns' own musical prowess, inspired Gabriel to work at becoming a composer.

In 1865, the year he graduated, Gabriel won first prize in composition for his *Cantique de Jean Racine*—a beautiful sacred work in French for chorus and organ—plus prizes in fugue and counterpoint. Gabriel's first church job was at Rennes, the capital of Brittany, but he returned to Paris in 1870, just in time for the Franco-Prussian War. On August 16 he left his organist position at Notre Dame de Clignancourt, after only a few months, to enlist in the army. Fauré was discharged in March 1871, and in October he became assistant organist to Charles-Marie Widor at the Church of Saint-Sulpice. During this time Fauré reconnected with his former teacher, Saint-Saëns, who introduced him to Parisian musical society. Saint-Saëns was principal organist at the Church of the Madeleine, but he was frequently absent on concert tours, so in 1874 Fauré was appointed as the Madeleine's deputy organist.

In January 1877 Fauré's Violin Sonata No. 1 premiered at a concert of the Société Nationale de Musique; this was a watershed for the composer, but it was not until the 1890s that Fauré's financial fortunes began to improve. In 1892 he was hired at the Paris Conservatoire as professor of composition, and in 1896 he became principal organist at the Madeleine. Finally, in 1905, Fauré became head of the Paris Conservatoire.

Fauré composed many works for piano, chamber ensemble, and orchestra, but his fame rests especially on his art songs—*mélodies*—and his Requiem. In *mélodies* such as *Lydia*, *Le secret*, *En sourdine*, and *Clair de lune*—the last three with lyrics by Paul Verlaine—Fauré established himself as probably the greatest composer of French art song.

One of Fauré's most beloved works is his Requiem, a staple of choirs—Catholic and non-Catholic—worldwide. Its beauty continues to move, although Fauré's spirituality was, at best, ambivalent. The ethereality of Fauré's Requiem would seem to derive from Fauré's vague desire for "rest," rather than a firmly held conviction of the truths of the Catholic faith.

Musicologist Carlo Caballero has posited that Fauré's attitudes to the Catholic faith cannot be definitively determined. In fact, the composer seemed intentionally to have avoided self-revelation on almost every topic. Caballero speculates that in his younger years Fauré was skeptical or agnostic, but that toward the end of his life he favored atheism. In any case, Fauré held cynicism toward the Catholic Church, and considered himself to be a freethinker (*libre-penseur*).

And why did Fauré compose the Requiem? It's not clear, but scholars speculate one impetus was the death of the composer's father in 1885. His mother died on New Year's Eve 1887, but by that time he was already at work on the Requiem.

There are several versions of Fauré's Requiem, as the composer made revisions based on professional needs. The original version dates from 1887 to 1888, and this was sung by the Madeleine boys' and mens' choir on January 16, 1888, at the funeral of a parishioner. The Madeleine's pastor did not care for Fauré's "*petit* Requiem," and opined that the parish did not have need of such music.

Fauré's orchestration emphasized darker colors, for along with the organ there was a string ensemble of violas and cellos only. The Introit (Requiem) begins solemnly in D minor, with the full choir. The key changes to B-flat major when the sopranos enter with *Te decet hymnus*, the text of the Introit verse, Psalm 65 (64):2. Instead of returning to the Requiem, the music goes directly into the Kyrie; this repeats the melody of the Requiem. The following three sections of the Requiem Mass, which Fauré did not set, are the Gradual (*Requiem æternam*), Sequence (*Dies irae*), and the Tract (*Absolve Domine*); these would have been sung in Gregorian chant.

In 1889 Fauré composed *Hostias*, a baritone solo, which is only the verse section of the Offertory antiphon. In the next year he composed the rest of the Offertory, *O Domine Jesu Christe.*

Commentators have noted the absence of the Sequence, *Dies iræ*. Unlike Mozart, Berlioz, and Verdi, Fauré did not set this dramatic text, which emphasizes God's judgment; he apparently desired to focus on the more comforting aspects of the Requiem Mass. Nevertheless, in a liturgical performance of the Requiem, the *Dies iræ* had to be chanted.

The Sanctus begins with the celestial songs of angels, which Fauré set for sopranos. It also features a solo violin, a change from the dark timbre of orchestral violas and cellos. Fauré did not set the Benedictus; instead, he set *Pie Jesu*, the final couplet of the *Dies iræ*, separately for soprano solo. There was a longstanding Parisian tradition of having *Pie Jesu* sung during the Elevation, in place of the Benedictus.

The Agnus Dei begins in F major, with a meltingly beautiful melody sung by the tenors. The second petition is more dramatic, sung by the whole choir to unstable, chromatic harmonies. The final petition—*Agnus Dei, qui tollis peccata mundi, dona eis requiem sempiternam*—returns to the original tenor melody. This transitions gracefully into the Communion antiphon, *Lux æterna*. The sopranos begin softly, on a single note C, which furnishes a common tone between F major and A-flat major, the new key. However, soon the harmonies change, the section ending on an A-major chord, which prepares for a return to the D-minor Requiem music from the Introit. But instead of ending in D minor, the section ends in D major, with the introductory music of the Agnus Dei played as an orchestral postlude.

In 1890, Fauré added the Responsory, *Libera me*, which he had composed in 1877. Strictly speaking, it is not part of the Mass but of the Burial Service, as is the sublime and childlike *In Paradisum*, which concludes the Requiem.

Throughout the late 1880s and early 1890s, when Fauré was composing his Requiem, his younger contemporary Claude Debussy (1862–1918) was laboring in the bohemian ambiance of Montmartre to discover his own musical voice. Finally, in 1894, came the premiere of Debussy's tone poem *Prélude à l'après-midi d'un faune* (*Prelude to the Afternoon of a Faun*), a work that effectively established his reputation as a composer and heralded the modern era in classical music.

Debussy is often cited as the first modern composer because of his strikingly new use of harmony and rhythm, which combined to produce a musical style dubbed Impressionism, in emulation of the style of painting. The Impressionists are admired for their atmospheric paintings in which small brushstrokes of different colors are juxtaposed—not blended—to produce a shimmering effect. The same could be said of Musical Impressionists, but in this case the small brushstrokes are colorful harmonies that do not follow traditional progressions. Since the seventeenth century, harmony in European music had had its foundation in triads—three-note major and minor chords. Debussy supplemented these to include chords built of four, five, and even six notes. He also allowed chordal movement of parallel fourths and fifths, an unacceptable sound in nineteenth-century harmony. Since his discovery of the Southeast Asian gamelan orchestra (all percussion instruments) at the Paris World Exposition of 1889, Debussy had been fascinated by non-Western scales and unconventional rhythms. The seven notes of the major and minor scales of Western music are built on a sequence of whole and half steps, but Debussy became interested in the whole-tone scale, which has only six notes and, as its name suggests, uses only whole steps, or whole tones. Through his interest in the early music movement and the Gregorian chant revival at the Abbey of Solesmes, Debussy also adopted the use of modal scales and harmonies. Add to these his innovative use of certain orchestral instruments. Debussy introduced more frequent use of unconventional wind instruments such as the *cor anglais*, and he often featured the flute. Within the strings he utilized special effects such as plucking (*pizzicato*) and mutes, along with an occasional solo passage as a striking orchestral color. Musical Impressionism also drew on textual influences from Symbolist poets—like Baudelaire, Mallarmé, and Verlaine—whose creed was to promote "absolute" truth through the use of indirect, symbolic language and free verse.

Throughout the years, even during his own lifetime, Maurice Ravel (1875–1937) was described as an imitator of Debussy and a practitioner of Musical Impressionism, yet both he and Debussy denied this. Although both composers employed an expanded palette of harmonic colors, rightly linked with Debussy's new and unique musical style, there are a few differences between the two. For one thing, Ravel tended to use strict, classical forms—like sonata form or Baroque dance forms—while Debussy had a freer approach.

During this era French musicians had an interest in the "ancient style," that is, music of the seventeenth and eighteenth centuries. This was associated with their desire to distance themselves from the overblown, emotional style of late Romantic German composers. French Baroque music, in their eyes, was more refined and delicate than German style. Ravel had always had an inclination toward "ancient style," and he strove for this in *Le Tombeau de Couperin*, named after François Couperin (1668–1733), the most illustrious member of a French musical dynasty. This suite for piano—four movements of which Ravel later orchestrated—follows a format typical of a suite of Baroque dances (Prélude, Fugue, Forlane, Rigaudon, Menuet, Toccata).

While the French word *tombeau* translates literally as "tomb," it means far more; in the seventeenth century it referred to a composition meant as a remembrance. Ravel dedicated each movement to the memory of a friend fallen in World War I. *Le Tombeau* opens with a lively (*Vif*) *Prélude* in 12/16 (6/8). Next comes a *Fugue* (*Allegro moderato*) in

4/4. The third dance, *Forlane* (*Furlana*), was originally from Italy but was imported to France in 1697 by the French composer André Campra. Its tempo, *Allegretto*, is spritely but not too fast, and it is typically in 6/8. After the preceding pieces, all in E minor, the *Rigaudon*, an animated duple meter dance, bursts out in a joyful C major. The fifth dance—in G major—is the *Menuet*, a more subdued courtly dance in triple meter. The final movement, *Toccata*, begins in E minor and is in a lively (*Vif*) duple meter. The earliest toccatas—from the seventeenth century—were improvisatory in style, but Ravel's seems to draw from the French organ tradition of the nineteenth and twentieth centuries, with its motor-like pattern of chords and fast, regular tempo.

Ravel, for all his interest in archaic styles, was also an admirer of jazz, the new style he had encountered during a 1928 U.S. tour. He later made references to jazz in some of his music, including his Piano Concerto in G.

24

The Russians—Twentieth Century

Each of the four Russian composers in this chapter lived at least part of his life during the Soviet era, but each had a different experience. Sergei Rachmaninov's prodigious musical gifts and his training prepared him to be composer, pianist, and conductor, but he rarely practiced all three professions simultaneously. After the disappointing premiere of his first symphony, Rachmaninov became depressed and stopped composing for four years. But in 1901 Sergei completed his second piano concerto and it premiered successfully, establishing his reputation as a composer. In 1904 Rachmaninov became a conductor at the Bolshoi Theatre. By the second year he was disenchanted as working conditions grew stressful because of the wider social unrest connected with the 1905 Revolution. Thus, in February 1906 he resigned and for the next several years the Rachmaninov family lived a nomadic existence in Italy, Germany, and America. In November 1909 Rachmaninov played his American recital debut at Smith College, Northampton, Massachusetts, and the premiere of his third piano concerto. The second performance—on January 16, 1910—was conducted by Gustav Mahler, then music director of the New York Philharmonic. In February the Rachmaninovs returned to Moscow until 1917. After witnessing the chaos leading to the October Revolution, Rachmaninov accepted an invitation to tour Scandinavia. He seized this opportunity to escape Russia with his family; on

December 22 they left by train from Saint Petersburg, arriving in Stockholm on December 24. While in Scandinavia Rachmaninoff received three offers from America, which he rejected. Later, however, he realized that America offered the best possibilities for supporting his family, so on November 1, 1918, the Rachmaninovs sailed for New York. Almost immediately he had a December recital in Providence, Rhode Island, which Rachmaninov played while recuperating from the Spanish flu.

The American years necessitated a heavy concert schedule for Rachmaninov, but such a punishing schedule left little time for composition. Thus, between 1918 and his death, Rachmaninov finished only six works—Piano Concerto No. 4 (1926), *Three Russian Songs* (1926), *Variations on a Theme of Corelli* (1931) for piano, *Rhapsody on a Theme of Paganini* (1934), Symphony No. 3 (1936), and *Symphonic Dances* (1940).

Although he was born only one year before Arnold Schoenberg, the "pioneer" of atonality, Rachmaninov's music is Romantic in style. One can hear in his earliest music echoes of Tchaikovsky, Musorgsky, Rimsky-Korsakov, and other Romantic Russians. Later, Rachmaninov advanced, but without abandoning his rich melodic and harmonic style.

Two other genres Rachmaninov cultivated were art song and liturgical music. Among his many beautiful songs, a special favorite is *Ne poy, krasatsiva prim ne* (Do not sing, my beauty, to me), with lyrics by Pushkin. Rachmaninov's Vespers (All-Night Vigil) is widely performed, and occasionally choirs sing separate sections, especially *Bogoroditsye Devo*, a setting of the Orthodox *Hail Mary*.

With Igor Stravinsky there is no doubt that he was a twentieth-century composer. Stravinsky was nine when he started piano lessons, but as with other composers his family wanted him to study law. In 1902 Stravinsky met Vladimir, a fellow law student who was Rimsky-Korsakov's youngest son. Igor asked Vladimir for an introduction to his father and the budding composer spent that summer with Rimsky-Korsakov's family. Rimsky advised Stravinsky not to study at Saint Petersburg Conservatory but to take private lessons with him. As Igor spent more and more time on music, he neglected his legal studies; thus, it became easy to quit law when his university was closed for two months after the "Bloody Sunday" riots of January 22, 1905.

In 1909 Stravinsky was approached by impresario Serge Diaghilev to compose three ballets for Diaghilev's Imperial Russian Ballet (*Ballets Russes*) in Paris. The first, based on a Russian fairytale, was *The Firebird* (*L'oiseau de feu*). It premiered in 1910 and was an instantaneous success. Stravinsky's fame increased as he composed the next two ballets for Diaghilev. The action of *Petrushka* (1911) happens during the Shrovetide Fair and is a tragic tale of three puppets in a lovers' triangle. Stravinsky's third ballet was *The Rite of Spring* (*Le sacre du printemps*), which premiered on May 29, 1913. The ballet's scenario—"Scenes of Pagan Russia"—was created by Diaghilev, who was capitalizing on the fad for "primitivism." The ballet's climax is a human sacrifice in which "the Chosen One," a teenage girl, dances herself to death. The scenario's topic was not "polite," nor was Stravinsky's music, as the young composer sought to shock with musical innovations—brutal rhythms with accents occurring in unexpected places over relentless rhythmic pulsations, clashing harmonies that juxtaposed two different keys simultaneously, repetitious melodic figures (ostinatos), and no traditional form or development. Instead, Stravinsky simply presented discrete masses of sound that are repeated seemingly randomly. Although the music is not atonal, it is not *in* any key; rather, it is *on* a key, revolving around one prominent note; this is sometimes called *neotonality*.

In 1924 Stravinsky returned to the Russian Orthodox faith he had discarded during his teens. One Catholic thinker who befriended the composer and encouraged him during this time was the neo-Thomist philosopher Jacques Maritain. In the 1920s Stravinsky moved from his primitive Russian style to a new style that came to be known as neo-classicism. Like the "ancient" style sometimes used by Ravel, it involves a return to Baroque forms and styles, as a rebellion against nineteenth-century German Romanticism. Stravinsky's neo-classical phase—which included both large and smaller works, such as the chamber work *Octuor* (*Octet*)—lasted until 1951, when his opera *The Rake's Progress* premiered. Two of Stravinsky's large neo-classical works include his opera-oratorio *Oedipus Rex* (1927) and *Symphony of Psalms* (1930), a setting of three Latin psalms for chorus and orchestra. *Oedipus Rex* was an adaptation for orchestra, chorus, and soloists of Sophocles' play. The French libretto was by Jean Cocteau, but Stravinsky had it translated into Latin by Jean Daniélou, S.J., later a cardinal and a *peritus* at the Second Vatican Council.

In his last creative period Stravinsky, now living in California, experimented with Arnold Schoenberg's twelve-tone system. However, Stravinsky did not slavishly follow Schoenberg's system; his music from this period still sounds *neotonal* and has many stylistic traits present in his music from the beginning.

Rachmaninov and Stravinsky both rejected the Russian Revolution and spent their lives in exile in America. Prokofiev and Shostakovich, however, spent most or all of their lives in the Soviet Union and both suffered at the hands of the Communists.

Initially Sergei Prokofiev (1891–1953) made his reputation as a radical modernist composer of highly dissonant music. He emigrated from Russia after the Revolution and lived in North America and Western Europe for eighteen years, during which he composed solo piano works and concertos for himself to play. The 1920s also saw the premieres of his opera *The Love for Three Oranges* (*L'Amour des trois oranges*) (1921), in Chicago, and some ballets commissioned by Diaghilev.

Once the Great Depression touched America and Western Europe, Prokofiev's opportunities diminished, so he began to consider returning to Russia. He had already been invited several times and had made exploratory visits, but it was not until 1936 that he moved with his family to the U.S.S.R. In the 1930s he composed several works commissioned by the Soviets, including *Lieutenant Kijé, Romeo and Juliet, Peter and the Wolf,* and *Alexander Nevsky*. These are among Prokofiev's best-known works, all of them displaying the melodiousness that would accord with the Soviet aesthetic of "Socialist Realism."

Alexander Nevsky was commissioned for Sergei Eisenstein's 1938 eponymous film. It tells the story of the thirteenth-century Russian hero Alexander Nevsky, who repelled Teutonic knights invading Russia. The climactic scene— cinematically and musically—is "The Battle on the Ice," in which the Germans ultimately break through the ice and fall into Lake Peipus. The film, assisted by Prokofiev's music, also presented a thinly veiled conflict between Soviet Russia and Nazi Germany. In 1939 Prokofiev reworked the film score into a cantata for mezzo soprano, chorus, and orchestra, and that is principally how *Alexander Nevsky* has come to be known.

In 1948 Prokofiev—and Shostakovich, along with other composers—was denounced by the government for "formalism." Formalism, as defined by a contemporary Soviet music dictionary was "the artificial separation of form from content and the conferring on form or its individual elements of a self-sufficient and primary importance to the detriment of content." Essentially, the Soviets opposed dissonant modern music with no patriotic Communist message.

With Dmitri Shostakovich (1906–1975) historical and personal events were intertwined so inextricably that his political allegiances were not always clear. Dmitri was eleven when the Revolution erupted and propelled Russia into seventy years of Communism; he was the first notable Russian composer to be trained within the Soviet system. In his teens Dmitri's idols were Stravinsky and Prokofiev, which did not please his composition professor. During his conservatory years Shostakovich saw the premiere of his first symphony; in 1927 it caught the attention of Bruno Walter, who conducted the symphony's Berlin premiere later that year. Leopold Stokowski also admired Shostakovich's first symphony; not only did he conduct the Philadelphia Orchestra in its American premiere (1928), but he also conducted the first recording.

In 1934 Shostakovich's opera *Lady Macbeth of the Mtsensk District* premiered in Leningrad. Initially the opera was successful both with the people and the government, but two years later Stalin attended a performance of *Lady Macbeth*. Shostakovich, who was present, was horrified to see Stalin's negative reaction. Several days later *Pravda* published an unsigned article, "Muddle Instead of Music," which described *Lady Macbeth* as a "deliberately dissonant, muddled stream of sounds … [that] quacks, hoots, pants, and gasps." Now pressure to recant was put on critics who had praised the opera. This slanderous campaign resulted in the December 11 premiere of his Fourth Symphony being cancelled by government officials. 1936 also marked the beginning of Stalin's Reign of Terror.

Shostakovich's Fifth Symphony premiered in 1937 and is thought to be his riposte to Stalin's condemnation of *Lady Macbeth* and the Fourth Symphony. The music of the Fifth was more accessible, and a newspaper statement purporting to be by Shostakovich described the work as "a Soviet artist's creative response to just criticism." Shostakovich's seeming capitulation to the party and his public statements praising the government led to his being discounted as a serious composer. Shostakovich then composed many patriotic works and wrote numerous patriotic essays using official Soviet jargon, so it seemed that he was a mouthpiece of the party. Or was he?

In 1979 things changed with the publication of Solomon Volkov's *Testimony: The Memoirs of Dmitri Shostakovich*. Volkov claimed to have published interviews and personal conversations revealing a hitherto unknown Shostakovich. Instead of being a willing collaborator with the Soviets, Shostakovich revealed his hatred of Stalin and indicated that his compositions contained coded references to Stalinist oppression. However, in 1980 American musicologist Laurel Fay published an article criticizing Volkov's *Testimony*.[1] She indicated that *Testimony* contained plagiarism, with eight sections taken from previously published articles by Shostakovich. Nevertheless, even though scholars argued over its authenticity, Volkov's *Testimony* was positively received by musicians and the concert-going public. Many friends of Shostakovich maintained that although Volkov's book had its weaknesses, it was true in many of its essentials.

In 1994 came a book corroborating much of Volkov's portrait of Shostakovich as dissimulating in his official words but revealing his true thoughts in his music. Elizabeth Wilson published *Shostakovich: A Life Remembered*, which contained reminiscences of the composer by friends and associates who now, in the post-Soviet era, could speak honestly. The Soviet regime was so horrific that Shostakovich evidently followed orders merely to survive. Knowing about Shostakovich's

---

1 Laurel Fay, "Shostakovich versus Volkov: Whose Testimony?" *Russian Review* 39, no. 4 (1980): 484–93. See also Laurel Fay, *Shostakovich: A Life* (Oxford University Press, 2000).

double life caused many to reevaluate his music and listen with new ears. His music, in its nonverbal way, represented his suffering. Whether or not one accepts Shostakovich's response to life under Communism, his best music has a depth that identifies him as one of the great twentieth-century composers.

25

English Masters:
Elgar and Vaughan Williams

In 1846 Saint George's Catholic Church, Worcester, hired twenty-year-old Protestant William Henry Elgar as organist/choirmaster. Two years later he married Ann Greening and they began their family. Possibly it was in 1852 at the birth of Lucy, their second child, that Ann Elgar entered the Catholic Church. Edward William Elgar, born on June 2, 1857, thus had a wholly Catholic upbringing. William also owned a music shop, which would provide Edward access to study scores. At about twelve Edward taught himself the violin; later he would have lessons, and eventually he scraped together funds to study with a teacher in London. In most other aspects of music, including composition, Elgar was self-taught. Probably his best school of composition was the time he spent as a professional violinist with William Stockley's orchestra in nearby Birmingham. The Church, too, offered Elgar opportunities to grow as a composer, as he helped his father and eventually became Saint George's organist in 1885.

Earlier—in 1849—Reverend John Henry Newman had founded the Oratory of Saint Philip Neri in Birmingham. It is not impossible that Elgar could have either met or played the violin in the presence of Newman, who was himself a violinist. In 1885 Cardinal Newman attended a concert conducted by Stockley in memory of Oratory School alumni.

All during this time Elgar was gaining recognition as a gifted provincial composer. With the premiere of his "Enigma" Variations in 1898, conducted by Hans Richter,[1] Elgar was "discovered" by the wider musical world.

Toward the end of 1898 Elgar had written to music publisher Novello with a proposal for the next Birmingham Triennial Festival, to be held in 1900. Elgar wrote: "I want to make this my chief work & to devote myself to it with something like a free mind."[2] It was over a year before he decided between a topic on the apostles and Newman's *The Dream of Gerontius*, which he had known at least since 1887. It was 1865 when Newman wrote *The Dream of Gerontius*, a long meditative poem on the passage of the Christian soul from death to everlasting life.

On January 1, 1900, a representative of the Birmingham Triennial Festival assured Elgar that *Gerontius* would be suitable, and the die was cast. A few weeks later the composer traveled to Birmingham Oratory to confer with Father William Neville, the late Cardinal Newman's executor, after correspondence in which Elgar suggested that the poem would need to be condensed for the musical setting. He assured Father Neville that he would "*not alter* anything & I should of course not omit anything peculiar to our Catholic point of view but w^d prefer to talk this over with you."[3]

The speed with which Elgar composed a work of such scope was amazing. The Birmingham premiere was set for October 3. On June 6 Elgar completed the vocal score, but on the eleventh the chorusmaster died and was replaced by

---

1   Richter had conducted the world premieres of Brahms' Symphonies Nos. 2 and 3, Bruckner's Symphonies 1, 3, 4, 8, and Wagner's *Ring* operas.

2   Quoted in Robert Anderson, *Elgar*, The Master Musicians (New York: Schirmer Books, 1993), 42.

3   Quoted in Percy M. Young, *Elgar, Newman, and The Dream of Gerontius: In the Tradition of English Catholicism* (London: Scolar Press, 1996), 115.

William Stockley, who came out of retirement to prepare the chorus. Richter, who was to conduct the premiere, received the full score of *Gerontius* only on September 23. The first performance was not worthy of Elgar's masterpiece, the chorus being especially inadequate. Elgar was depressed; nevertheless, not all the critics panned *Gerontius*. Some could discern a masterpiece, and opined that despite its poor rendition, "no composition by an Englishman equals it in sheer technique, to say nothing of real poetic feeling."[4] In Düsseldorf Julius Buths recognized the greatness of *Gerontius*, which led to its performance there in December 1901. This, and subsequent English performances of higher caliber, eventually led to the public's realization that *Gerontius* was, indeed, a true masterpiece.

In his musical interpretation of Saint John Henry Newman's poem, Elgar sought to portray vividly the progress of an old man, Gerontius,[5] from his deathbed to the threshold of eternal life. He knew that for the title role to have the dramatic verisimilitude that would do justice to Newman's concept, Gerontius would have to be

> a man like us not a priest or a saint, but a *sinner*, a repentant one of course but still no end of a *worldly man* in his life, & now brought to book. Therefore I've not filled his part with Church tunes & rubbish but a good, healthy full-blooded romantic, remembered worldliness, so to speak.[6]

The Dream of Gerontius begins with a ten-minute orchestral prelude that presents all musical motives that will figure prominently. In Part I Gerontius (a tenor), at death's door, sings wearily, in quasi-recitative style, of his dread of death.

---

4   Baughan, *Morning Leader, 4 October*, quoted in Robert Anderson, *Elgar*, Master Musicians, 47.
5   The name "Gerontius" is derived from the Greek *geron*, for "old man."
6   Quoted in Young, *Elgar*, 118.

Surrounded by his friends, who implore God's mercy and the intercession of the saints, Gerontius sings an aria, *Sanctus fortis*, which affirms his faith in Christ and His Church. The aria, in triple meter (perhaps symbolizing the Trinity), features the lyrics of Newman's hymn, "Firmly I believe and truly." Part I ends with the appearance of the Priest, a bass, who summons Gerontius with the words, "Proficiscere, anima Christiana, de hoc mundo! Go forth upon thy journey, Christian soul! Go, in the Name of God . . . ." Part I of Elgar's oratorio comprises Section 1 of Newman's poem, and cuts the least from the poem.

Elgar's Part II comprises Newman's Sections 2–7, and this is where Elgar made the most extensive cuts. In Part II the Angel appears to the Soul (Gerontius, now dead). In the original poem, Newman had portrayed the Angel as male, but Elgar decided to assign the role to a mezzo-soprano, so he deleted all but two references to the Angel as male.

The Guardian Angel conducts the Soul to the Court of Judgment, where they are met by a chorus of demons. Elgar depicts their "sullen howl" with a fugal setting in which their shrill voices mock the Soul and try to divert him from his heavenward goal. The Angel strengthens the Soul and prepares him for Purgatory. As the Angel sings of "the flame of the Everlasting Love," that "doth burn ere it transform," a Choir of Angelicals, "least and most childlike of the sons of God," is heard singing "Praise to the Holiest in the height." The Soul and his Guardian Angel pass into the House of Judgment. The Angel of the Agony (bass) appears and sings a final intercessory prayer. Voices on earth repeat the earlier intercessions of Part I, and Souls in Purgatory sing the words of Psalm 90 (89):1–2. The Guardian Angel "softly and gently" commits the Soul to Purgatory as the Souls continue their entreaty and Angelicals conclude with their song of praise.

Despite its Catholic theology, Newman's poem had achieved a wide acceptance, perhaps because of the widely publicized annotations of General Gordon of Khartoum. The general, a devout evangelical Anglican, had annotated his own copy of *The Dream* before his death in Egypt. As the poem had brought comfort to him, so it found a place in the hearts of many non-Catholics. Perhaps this contributed to the Birmingham Festival's endorsement of Elgar's use of such a Catholic text for his contribution to the festival. Even non-Catholics were won over by the heartfelt power and beauty of the music. Two years later, however, when *Gerontius* was to be performed in Worcester Cathedral at the Three Choirs Festival—which rotates among the cathedrals of Worcester, Gloucester, and Hereford—Protestant members of the Festival Committee suggested some word omissions in *Gerontius*. For this occasion, the composer and the Birmingham Oratory agreed to the changes. By this time, though, the work's success was so assured that even non-Catholics took umbrage, as witnessed by the comments of J. A. Fuller Maitland, who recalled that "the soloists were required ... to mumble the name 'Maria' at the beginning of the tenor solo, and at the words 'and masses on the earth and prayers in heaven' the representative of the angel must sing the first words with closed lips."[7]

Elgar donated his autograph manuscript of the score to the Birmingham Oratory, and concluded his dedicatory letter, saying: "I must add that nothing would give me greater happiness than to feel that the work, into which I put my whole soul, sh^d be in its original form, near to where the sacred author of the poem made his influence felt."[8]

Another composer often featured at the Three Choirs Festival was Ralph Vaughan Williams (1872–1958). His hymn tunes (e.g., *Sine nomine, Down Ampney, Kingsfold, King's Lynn, Forest Green*) are beloved even now, and many of his

7   Ibid., 132.
8   Ibid., 129.

sacred choral works have become concert and church standards. Some of Vaughan Williams' hymn tunes are original (*Sine nomine*), while others were folksongs that he adapted as hymns. The energy he devoted to these hymns was part of the project of the *English Hymnal*, published in 1906, and edited by Percy Dearmer, an Anglican clergyman. Vaughan Williams was the music editor for the hymnal, and the high musical quality of its contents is very much thanks to him. He considered his work on the *English Hymnal* to be one of the most valuable experiences of his creative life: "But I know now … that two years of close contact with some of the best (as well as some of the worst) tunes in the world was a better musical education than any amount of sonatas and fugues."[9] One later work by Vaughan Williams that uses an actual folksong is his *Five Variants of Dives and Lazarus*, for harp and string orchestra, which was commissioned for the 1939 New York World's Fair. *Dives and Lazarus* is an English folksong that Vaughan Williams had earlier converted into a hymn tune—*Kingsfold*—for the *English Hymnal*. Catholics today know it as the melody for "I heard the voice of Jesus say." In addition, the composer used this melody in his *English Folksong Suite*.

A second influence on Vaughan Williams was music of the Tudor era. His first work to illustrate this was *Fantasia on a Theme of Thomas Tallis*, which premiered at the 1910 Three Choirs Festival, held that year at Gloucester Cathedral. For those who wonder about the "theme," it is one of eight melodies—one in each of the eight church modes plus a ninth melody to go with "Come Holy Ghost"—that Tallis composed for a collection of metrical psalms compiled in 1567 for Matthew Parker, the first Protestant archbishop of Canterbury. Because the translations were metrical, any psalm could

---

9   Quoted in Pakenham, Simona, *Ralph Vaughan Williams: A Discovery of His Music* (London: MacMillan, 1957), 124.

be sung to any of the eight melodies. Tallis' melody chosen by Vaughan Williams was the "Third Mode Melody"; that is, it is in the third (Phrygian) mode and was printed with the words of Psalm 2, "Why fumeth in sight the gentiles spite?" At the back of Archbishop Parker's Psalter, Tallis listed all eight melodies by their "Nature" (i.e., their *ethos*), for example, "The third doth rage, and roughly brayth." All eight psalms are printed in four-part harmony and the melody is in the tenor voice, a common practice in Tallis' day. Vaughan Williams also included Tallis' melody in the *English Hymnal*, where its tune name is *Third Mode Melody*. Vaughan Williams scored his *Fantasia* for two string orchestras and a string quartet. It was well received and continues to be popular to this day.

Among his many orchestral and vocal works influenced by—but not using—English folksong is Vaughan Williams' short "Romance," *The Lark Ascending*. The violin solo portrays the exalted flight of a lark as it circles and soars over the landscape, represented by the accompaniment. Its melody follows the contours of folk melody—reminiscent of Gregorian modes and the pentatonic scale (found on the black keys of the piano). The original 1914 version was for violin and piano, but Vaughan Williams rescored the accompaniment for orchestra after World War I and that had its premiere in 1921. Ever since, it has been a listener favorite.

26

France in the Mid-Twentieth Century

Three French composers who were born just before World War I—and thus lived their creative lives beginning in the interwar years—are the subject of this chapter. While Fauré, Debussy, and Ravel had no meaningful connection with the Catholic Church, these younger composers were, or became, fervent Catholics.

Not far from Rouen, medieval capital of Normandy, is Louviers, the birthplace of Maurice Duruflé, organ virtuoso and composer of a small but revered body of works. In 1902, when Maurice was born, it had been less than a decade since Claude Monet painted his series of twenty-six views of Rouen Cathedral seen at different times of day. A decade later Maurice's parents would enroll him as a boarder at the cathedral's choir school.

Central to Maurice's musical experience as a cathedral chorister was Gregorian chant. In 1903 Pope Saint Pius X had issued his *motu proprio* on sacred music (*Tra Le Sollecitudini*), in which Gregorian chant and sacred polyphony were promoted. By the time Maurice became a chorister at Rouen Cathedral, the Solesmes monks' restoration of chant to its ancient purity had already been incorporated into the cathedral's musical life.

At seventeen Maurice became organist at his home parish in Louviers. It was then that he began commuting to Paris for lessons with organist-composer Charles Tournemire (1870–1939), in preparation for the Conservatoire's entrance examination. Duruflé successfully passed the exam and was admitted to the organ class of Eugène Gigout (1844–1925), one of the pioneers of incorporating Gregorian chant into French organ music. His composition professor was Paul Dukas (1865–1935), best known as the composer of *The Sorcerer's Apprentice* (*L'apprenti sorcier*). While Duruflé's melodies are influenced by Gregorian chant, his harmonic language pays homage to Dukas, and to the music of Debussy and Ravel. Duruflé was a stellar student, winning first prizes in every subject.

In 1930 Duruflé began his tenure as organist at the Parisian church of Saint-Étienne-du-Mont. During the 1940s Duruflé substituted as organ professor for his former teacher Marcel Dupré, who was away on tour, and it was during this time that he met the brilliant organ student Marie-Madeleine Chevalier. They were married in 1953, and from that year until 1975 they shared the post at Saint-Étienne-du-Mont.

Duruflé's music is a small collection of precious jewels. His list of compositions comprises only fourteen, as he was a perfectionist and was always revising his work. Like his organ music, Duruflé's choral music makes use of Gregorian chant. In his Requiem, composed in 1947, almost every movement is directly based upon chants from the Requiem Mass.

Duruflé provided three different accompaniments for his Requiem. The original version used a large orchestra; he also published a version accompanied by organ alone. The third version, published in 1961, is for a small orchestra of organ, twenty-two strings, and optional parts for harp, two or three trumpets, and two, three, or four timpani. The chant-based melodies with their subtle and free rhythms, the masterful counterpoint, modal harmonies, and Duruflé's colorful orchestration combine to make his Requiem a deeply spiritual, moving work by a fervent believer.

Duruflé also composed four motets on Gregorian themes; *Ubi caritas* is based on the chant traditionally sung on Maundy Thursday. *Tota pulchra es* is for women's voices and uses three of five psalm antiphons from Second Vespers of the Immaculate Conception. *Tu es Petrus* is a rousing, contrapuntal setting of the fifth antiphon from First Vespers for the Feast of Saints Peter and Paul. Finally, *Tantum ergo* is the familiar Benediction hymn.[1]

Like many musicians and lovers of sacred music, the Duruflés were unhappy with the unwarranted abandonment of Gregorian chant after Vatican II. In 1966 Duruflé composed his *Messe "cum jubilo"*—for unison choir of baritones, with organ—based on the Gregorian Mass IX (*cum jubilo*). Perhaps this was Duruflé's way of continuing the Gregorian tradition in the wake of the domination of liturgical music by secular commercial music styles. However, his final opus was *Notre Père*, a French setting of the Our Father, composed for the parishioners of Saint-Étienne-du-Mont. While Duruflé's musical style was thought by some to be retrospective and out of step with the atonal avant-garde, nevertheless, his use of timeless Gregorian chant, coupled with a love for beauty and his strong faith, have assured him a permanent place in the heritage of sacred music.

At first glance Francis Poulenc (1899–1963) may not seem to be the composer to create one of the twentieth century's greatest operas on a religious subject. Up until 1936 he was known more as a composer of music infused with the styles of dance hall and cabaret, but in that year everything changed. A good friend was killed in a car accident; this tragedy turned Poulenc toward God, and he returned to the practice of his Catholic faith. After composing several sacred choral works,

---

1   Its text is stanzas 5 and 6 of Saint Thomas Aquinas' *Pange lingua gloriosa*.

Poulenc decided to compose an opera on a religious theme. It took the composer three years to complete the score of *Dialogues des Carmélites*, which premiered in 1957. The libretto is based on the true story of the Martyrs of Compiègne, sixteen Carmelite nuns who were guillotined in 1794 during the Reign of Terror. They were canonized in 1906 by Pope Saint Pius X.

The dialogues, which are the backbone of the opera, show the character development of Blanche as she becomes Sister Blanche of the Agony of Christ. Each dialogue contributes to her transformation, but the words of Sister Constance, Blanche's fellow novice, provide the key to a major theme of the story—the transfer of grace. Sister Constance tells Blanche: "We do not die for ourselves alone, but for, or instead of, each other." This concept eventually allows Blanche to rejoin her sisters at the scaffold, after having fled from the prospect of such a gruesome death.

The opera's final scene opens with an orchestral prelude in which the texture is amplified by menacing, dissonant brass chords. Percussion instruments suggest the marching of soldiers, the gathering of the crowd, and the rolling of the tumbril. Suddenly this stops and quiet woodwind chords introduce the *Salve Regina*.[2] At the first descent of the guillotine on the neck of the first sister, the singing becomes louder, and the crowd sings along with the nuns. As each sister is guillotined, the nuns' singing is diminished, voice by voice. Seeing Blanche approach from the crowd, Sister Constance smiles at her and then goes to her death. Blanche finishes with the doxology "Deo Patri gloria / Et Filio qui a mortuis / Surrexit ac Paraclito / In saeculorum saecula, / In saeculorum." Her voice is silenced; the crowd begins to disperse; the music ends quietly. It is one of the most moving conclusions to an opera, a fitting representation of the transfer of grace.

---

2   Not the Gregorian chant, but an original melody by Poulenc.

What does the music of Eternity sound like? One composer—one of the few—who tried to portray Eternity through concert music was Olivier Messiaen (1908–1992). In the increasingly secular twentieth century, Messiaen sought to reveal the sublimity, the vastness, the depths, the tenderness, the anguish, the joy, the clarity, and the mystery of Catholicism to a world that did not care to be reminded of its own finiteness and apostasy. Musically, Messiaen did this in ways that produced varying reactions (awe, disgust, contemplation, delight) in his listeners. Messiaen's musical language combines diverse elements of modern music—clashing dissonance, irregular rhythms, and jagged melodies—with such traditional elements as Gregorian chant and tonal harmony.

When he was eleven, Messiaen began studies at the Paris Conservatoire and won many prizes. His harmony professor noticed Olivier's gift for improvisation and encouraged him to study organ with organist-composer-improviser Marcel Dupré. Prior to this Messiaen had never played the organ, but it was to become his main instrument, and at twenty-two he became principal organist at the Church of the Holy Trinity. Here he would be at the organ almost every Sunday for the rest of his life.

Already in 1927, with *Le banquet céleste* (*The Heavenly Banquet*), certain signposts of the Eternal manifested themselves. Although only twenty-five measures long, *Le banquet céleste* is meant to last for six minutes. Messiaen indicated that the work was to be "very slow, ecstatic," and this he effected by using sustained chords; the first chord, for example, takes seven seconds to change. The listener loses all sense of meter and time because of each chord's length. The key signature of *Le banquet céleste* indicates F-sharp major, a key that Messiaen frequently used to symbolize God. Messiaen composed almost no liturgical polyphony, except for his motet *O sacrum convivium*. Commentators have offered various reasons, but it would seem that for him the only true liturgical music was Gregorian chant.

When World War II began, Messiaen was drafted, but because of poor vision he was assigned as a medical auxiliary. In May 1940 Messiaen was captured and interned at a German prison camp. There he encountered three musicians—a violinist, a clarinetist, and a cellist—for whom Messiaen composed a trio that became the nucleus of *Quartet for the End of Time* (*Quatuor pour la fin du temps*), one of his most famous works. The eight-movement *Quatuor* was premiered in January 1941 for an audience of five thousand prisoners; the cello had only three strings and the piano was an old upright with keys that stuck. The inscription on the quartet's score reads: "In homage to the angel of the Apocalypse, who raises a hand toward heaven saying: 'There shall be time no longer.'"

In the spring of 1941 Messiaen was released from the Stalag and upon his return to France began teaching harmony at the Conservatoire. Messiaen's most monumental work of the 1940s was his *Turangalîla-Symphonie*. The *Turangalîla-Symphonie* is one of Messiaen's three works inspired by the Tristan and Isolde legend, and although it concerns human love Messiaen considered that human love was but a mirror of divine love.

Birdsong had been part of his music since the 1930s as a generalized feature, but after *Quatuor pour la fin du temps* Messiaen increasingly represented specific species of birds and the 1950s became a time of intense focus on birdsong. Not only was Messiaen interested in ornithology; he also saw birds as "little servants of immaterial joy,"[3] akin to angels in their capacity as messengers of God.

During the 1960s and early 1970s, Messiaen composed some works of immense size. Among them, *La Transfiguration*

---

3   Olivier Messiaen, trans. John Satterfield, *Technique de ma langage musical* (*The Technique of My Musical Language*), vol. 1 (Paris: Alphonse Leduc, 1956), p. 34.

de Notre-Seigneur Jésus-Christ is a *Summa* of Messiaen's vocation to praise God's glory and to bring liturgy into the concert
hall. The work is for seven instrumental soloists, a one-hundred-
voice mixed chorus, and large orchestra. The lyrics are in Latin,
from the Gospel narrative of the Transfiguration, interspersed
with other Scripture passages, liturgical texts of the Feast of the
Transfiguration, and Aquinas' *Summa Theologiæ.*

Messiaen's only opera, *Saint-François d'Assise,* took eight
years to complete and premiered in Paris in 1983. It too is
monumental—lasting over four hours—with a very large
orchestra, a 150-voice chorus, and seven principal singers.
Rather than a narrative biography of Saint Francis, eight tab-
leaux chart Francis' spiritual development. Some of Messiaen's sources were the *Fioretti,* the *Considerations on the Holy
Stigmata,* and Francis's *Canticle to the Sun.* For Messiaen
Saint Francis was the personage most like Christ, and therefore likely to be most convincing onstage. Each tableau ends
with a miracle, illustrative of what the composer termed the
"progression of grace."

Truth is the theme of *Saint-François d'Assise.* In Tableau
5 Messiaen paraphrases Saint Thomas: "God dazzles us by
excess of Truth. Music leads us to God for lack of Truth."[4]
Through his unique and dazzling music, Messiaen attempted
to flood our darkened world with the glory of God shining on
the face of Jesus Christ. The growing interest in Messiaen's
music means that the truths of the Catholic faith will reach
more souls through concerts and recordings of his music, so
long as we are ready to explain them and not allow them to
be diffused into the general aura of "spirituality" that has sur-
faced in recent years.

---

4   Translation from Camille Crunelle Hill, "Saint Thomas Aquinas and the Theme of Truth
in Messiaen's *Saint François d'Assise,*" in *Messiaen's Language of Mystical Love,* ed. Siglind Bruhn
(New York and London: Garland Publishing, 1998), 143.

27

The Americans

"I hear America singing, the varied carols I hear," wrote Walt Whitman in 1860. America's music has indeed been varied throughout its history. Long before the Pilgrims published the *Bay Psalm Book* in 1640, Spanish missionaries had already been teaching Latin chants to Native Americans throughout *Nueva España*.

The complete history of America begins not with the Pilgrims in 1620, nor Jamestown in 1607, but with Columbus in 1492 and the Spanish explorers, including Franciscan missionaries. Conventional histories show the history of a Protestant nation and America's Catholic roots are forgotten. This chapter will provide an introduction to music in the Catholic foundation of American history, along with development of an American musical style within the Protestant narrative of American history. Lastly, we'll look at music that has become iconic of America but is by first-generation American composers.

Starting with the voyages of Christopher Columbus, the faith was practiced on shipboard. The captain officiated at morning and evening prayers, and these included the chanting of litanies and the *Salve Regina*. This was before the introduction of Mass, when a priest was on board during Columbus' final voyage (1502–1506).

The Church encouraged European musicians to immigrate to *Nueva España*. Once in America, these musicians served three different populations—Indians (Native Americans), Mestizos (children of Indian and Spanish parents), and Creoles (children born in America of Spanish parents)—these were trained as performers and composers. The Church also established schools to form the Indians in the Catholic faith, and to teach them arts and manners. One notable missionary was Pedro de Gante (Peter of Ghent, ca. 1480–1572), a lay Franciscan. Pedro established in Mexico a school that prioritized music in order to attract Indian students. After the Franciscans, Dominicans arrived in 1526 and Augustinians in 1532. Beginning in 1572, Jesuit missionaries were also active in teaching and promoting music. Because of the Indians' aptitude and love for music—they easily learned Gregorian chant and European polyphony—all these missionaries found that music was an effective tool for evangelization.

The first printed music book in the New World was an *Ordinarium Missae*, printed in Mexico City in 1556. From 1558 to 1589, a Mexico City press published thirteen liturgical books with music, twelve more than appeared in Madrid during the same time period. Music of Spanish composers, especially Morales and Victoria, featured prominently in Mexico during the sixteenth and seventeenth centuries, but there were also native-born and other Spanish composers; one was Juan de Lienas (fl. ca. 1617–1654). It is not certain whether he was born in Spain or Mexico, but his surviving music was all composed for the use of nuns at Mexico City's *Convento del Carmen*. One example of Lienas' polyphony is *Coenantibus autem illis*, whose text is from Matthew 26:26 and is used for the Divine Office (Matins of Corpus Christi). Just as Palestrina and his contemporaries did, Lienas sets each line of text as a new point of imitation.

Lyrics	Translation	Points of Imitation
Coenantibus autem illis,	And whilst they were at supper,	Point 1
accepit Iesus panem,	Jesus took bread,	Point 2
et benedixit ac fregit,	and blessed, and broke,	Point 3
deditque discipulis suis:	and gave it to his disciples, and said:	Point 4
Accipite, et manducate:	Take ye, and eat:	Point 5
Hoc est enim corpus meum.	This is my body.	Point 6

In the final phrase (Point 6), the vocal texture is completely homophonic, that is, with no imitation, in order to highlight the doctrinal centrality of Christ's words: "This is my body."

In addition to the Native Americans, African slaves were also prominent in public celebrations, both sacred and secular. Franciscan friar Toribio de Benavente Motolinía (1490–1569) documented the participation of large groups of Mexican Indian musicians in Corpus Christi and Easter Week.

Because the official history of America originates with English Puritans and the development of the British colonies, American history is usually seen through an English Protestant lens. After the War of Independence, eighteenth-century American composers such as William Billings (1746–1800) and Francis Hopkinson (1737–1791), a signer of the Declaration of Independence, delighted their compatriots with music of character and elegance. The multitudes of immigrants who came to America throughout the years brought with them their music, both cultivated and traditional. Although the immigrants were of many nationalities and ethnicities, the dominant body of folk music came from English traditions. Anglo-American folk songs were (and are) popular, but also a rich tradition of folk hymns developed. For example, the shape-note hymns published in such hymnals as the *Sacred Harp* (1844) and *Southern Harmony* (1835) were an important part of Protestant hymn singing in the South. Many hymns of this sort came to be known as "white spirituals," after musicologist George Pullen Jackson coined the term—in his 1938 book *White Spirituals in the Southern Uplands*—as counterparts to Negro spirituals.

When Czech composer Antonín Dvořák was asked where Americans could find authentic sources of a truly American music, he recommended African American and Native American melodies.[1] Dvořák, renowned for using Czech dance forms and melodies in his own music, discovered Negro spirituals through his African American student Harry T. Burleigh (1866–1949), a fine classical singer and composer in his own right. Dvořák encouraged Burleigh to make spirituals more widely known, and this is what he did. Burleigh was the first to arrange the unison melodies of the slaves into choral and solo settings that clothed them in classical harmonies. Indeed, it is thanks to Burleigh's efforts, and those of other arrangers, that Negro spirituals remain a beloved part of choral concerts and of American musical culture generally.

As composers searched for a uniquely American style of music, a small group of New Englanders emerged in the late nineteenth century. Among them were George Whitefield Chadwick, Charles Martin Loeffler, and Edward McDowell, all of whom were influenced by European masters. They

---

1   See Chapter 21 above.

were eclipsed, however, when later tastemakers found what they considered to be true American composers, untainted by European influences.

In the 1930s the music of Charles Ives (1874–1954) gradually began to be discovered, and young composers such as Virgil Thomson (1896–1989) and Aaron Copland (1900–1992) began introducing American folksong themes into their music. Charles Ives (1874–1954) is considered by many to be the first truly American composer, and he fits the conventional historical trajectory of the East Coast Protestant. Born in Danbury, Connecticut, Ives grew up in the Congregationalist tradition, with influences from New England Transcendentalism. As a boy he sang and played on the organ most of the popular Protestant hymns of the day, which he would later incorporate into his own music. Ives' father was the town bandmaster, so Charles grew up with the sound of band music in his ears. As an undergraduate at Yale, Charles studied composition with Horatio Parker (1863–1919), who had been a student of Chadwick and who had also studied in Munich with Josef Rheinberger, a Catholic. But while Charles was learning the European style, he was experimenting and going down new musical paths. Ives preceded some of the European avant-garde composers, like Arnold Schoenberg, with his use of certain dissonant musical techniques. After Yale, Charles founded Ives and Myrick, an insurance company that became an industry leader in instituting now-standard insurance practices. In his leisure, however, Ives continued to compose in his unique style, which blended European classical music with Protestant hymnody, American popular music, and experimental techniques. His 1914 song, "General William Booth Enters into Heaven," is an example of his style incorporating these influences. The lyrics are excerpts from Vachel Lindsay's poem about the founder of the Salvation Army. Lindsay's poem quotes a refrain from the Protestant hymn, "Are you washed in the Blood of the Lamb," and Ives inserts phrases from a popular hymn tune used with these lyrics. The song's cumulative form leads at the end to an entire stanza of the hymn, "There Is a Fountain Filled with Blood." Ives' music was not widely known, and his influence was not felt until after World War II. He could justifiably be called the founder of the experimental-music tradition in the United States.

Jazz, another music that sprang from African American roots, was influential on two American composers. George Gershwin (1898–1937), born of Ukrainian-Russian Jewish immigrants, grew up in Brooklyn, New York. He began piano lessons at age ten, and when George left high school at fourteen he began working as a song plugger, a pianist who plays new songs in order to entice customers into buying the sheet music. The year 1916 was the year of Gershwin's first published song, and it was only three years later when his song "Swanee" became a nationwide hit. Around that time Gershwin began composing musical comedies; in 1924 his brother Ira joined him as lyricist and they inaugurated a series of hit shows, including *Lady Be Good* (1924), *Oh, Kay!* (1926), *Funny Face* (1927), *Strike up the Band* (1927 and 1930), *Girl Crazy* (1930), and *Of Thee I Sing* (1931), which was the first Pulitzer Prize–winning musical.

Gershwin, however, yearned to compose classical music that would blend classical and jazz styles. His opportunity came when popular danceband leader Paul Whiteman invited Gershwin to compose something for a concert at New York's Aeolian Hall. The premiere of *Rhapsody in Blue* was on February 12, 1924, with Gershwin at the piano accompanied by Whiteman's Palais Royal Orchestra, a jazz band with added strings; Whiteman's arranger Ferde Grofé orchestrated the work. Although *Rhapsody* did not please all critics, it was a success with the audience and has been a popular concert piece ever since. Another Gershwin work baffling to critics was *Porgy and Bess*, which premiered in 1935. Critics were divided; was it an opera or a musical comedy? Did it belong at the Met, or on Broadway? Gershwin himself considered *Porgy and Bess* a "folk opera." Not until 1976 did it find a secure place as an opera, when Houston Grand Opera produced the full version of Gershwin's score.

The music of Aaron Copland (1900–1990) seems so iconic of America that it's hard to believe he was the son of Russian Jewish immigrants. Copland's most well-known music is evocative of the wide-open spaces of America, yet he—like Gershwin—grew up in the urban landscape of Brooklyn.

Copland's musical path was classical from the beginning, though he would also incorporate jazz elements into his music. More important to Copland's enduring reputation, however, was his use of American folk song as raw material in many of his compositions. In 1921 Copland became the first of a succession of young American composers to study composition with the esteemed pedagogue Nadia Boulanger (1887–1979) in Paris, where he imbibed the crisp, dissonant, and rhythmically vibrant style of Stravinsky.

Copland returned to America in 1924 and began trying to make a living as a composer. During the Great Depression Copland became active in leftist politics. It seems that this activism was at bottom a search for his own musical style, for his "tour" of Populism, Socialism, and Communism put him in touch with the American folk revival, which had been facilitated by the folk song researches of John Lomax and his son Alan, among others. All these social and musical impulses coalesced during the 1930s into an artistic choice that would make Copland's music America's "signature-tune." He saw that the modernist musical style he had been using was not financially rewarding and that a simpler, more populist style would be better both for him and for America. In the late 1930s Copland began composing ballets, among them some of his most popular works, in this new style. *Billy the Kid* (1939) was first, with *Rodeo* (1942) and *Appalachian Spring* (1944)—which won the Pulitzer Prize—following, all to huge acclaim. All of these incorporate folk melodies and harmonies that are a mixture of dissonant, jazzy, and consonant. Aaron Copland's music is popular to this day, and for many Americans it is emblematic of the United States.

28

Three Holy Minimalists and a Mystic Scot

The so-called Holy Minimalists are a group of composers active in the late twentieth and early twenty-first centuries known for their concert music with spiritual themes. First, a word about minimalism before we define *Holy* Minimalism. Minimally defined, minimalism is a musical style that features tonal harmony and much repetition of rhythmic and melodic patterns. It developed in New York in the 1960s; two of its best-known composers are Steve Reich and Philip Glass. Because minimalist-like traits are present in the works of Henryk Górecki (1933–2010), Arvo Pärt (b. 1935), and John Tavener (1944–2013)—all Christians—these composers came to be known as Holy Minimalists.

Before 1993 Górecki was little known outside his native Poland, but by September of that year a recording of his Symphony No. 3 (*Symphony of Sorrowful Songs*) had sold four hundred thousand-plus copies. Górecki's symphony was not new, however; composed in 1976, it is a landmark in the creative life of a man rooted in the faith and culture of rural Poland, a man who—like Saint John Paul II—lived through illness, loss, and the cataclysmic Nazi and Communist eras.

After Stalin's death in 1953, Polish composers achieved access to musical influences from Western Europe. Górecki's compositions from his student days through the 1960s show selective use of atonality and serialism. Concurrently the composer pursued an interest in earlier Polish music, as in his 1969 orchestral work *Old Polish Music*.

In the 1970s Górecki began to retreat from his dissonant harmonic style. The human voice became more important, either as a component of instrumental works like the Second and Third Symphonies or in choral works like *Euntes ibant et flebant* (1972) and *Amen* (1975). This melodic element, plus the composer's continuing interest in earlier Polish music, brought a more consonant sound and a more emotional and spiritual element to his music. The Third Symphony (*Symphony of Sorrowful Songs*) has three movements, each in a slow tempo and each featuring a soprano solo sung to lyrics of lament and supplication. The first lyric is a late fifteenth-century lament of the Blessed Virgin for her crucified Son; the second is a prayer scratched on the wall of a Gestapo prison by an eighteen-year-old girl, and the third is a mother's lament for her son slain in a rebellion.

Górecki's compositions of the 1980s and beyond continued on the consonant, spiritual pathway, while still incorporating music from Polish folk traditions. Two outstanding choral works from the 1980s are *Miserere* and *Totus tuus.* An explicitly political statement, Górecki's *Miserere* was his response to violence perpetrated in Bydgoszcz against Rural Solidarity demonstrators by two hundred militiamen on March 19, 1981. The text consists of only the words "Domine Deus noster, Miserere nobis." The radiant *Totus tuus* (1987) was composed for John Paul II's third visit to Poland. The lyrics by Maria Boguslawska are inspired by the pope's motto, and the homophonic texture, with its mesmerizing, repeated, triadic sonorities, reveals Górecki's indebtedness to Polish church music and Marian devotion. With his music Górecki brought his Catholic faith out of the private sphere and into the public; he was a composer whose numinous music is an antidote to the brutality and ugliness of today's secularized world.

In this world of noise pollution there is need for silence, yet many seem not to realize this. Silence is that precious state that allows one to encounter God and to hear His voice. The music of Estonian composer Arvo Pärt is born of such silence, and it bespeaks a vastness that is both an emptiness shorn of all excess and an amplitude containing everything.

The signal event of 1953 was Josef Stalin's death. Oppression was lifted, but Soviet restrictions on music were still somewhat in force. In 1954 Pärt began to study piano, theory, analysis, music literature, and folk music at Tallinn's Music Middle School (equivalent to an undergraduate college). He had been composing since age fourteen or fifteen, and by seventeen had already had a work performed publicly. After a break as a military oboist and drummer, Pärt returned to the middle school to complete his courses before entering Tallinn Conservatory in the fall of 1957. Pärt's earliest works were in a tonal, neo-classical style, which served him well when he began composing film scores.

In the early 1960s little atonal and twelve-tone music by Western Europeans was known in Estonia as it had long been forbidden in the U.S.S.R. Yet somehow Pärt acquired scores to study and he began to compose in twelve-tone style. Throughout the 1960s Pärt made concessions to Soviet taste by composing tonal, cheerful compositions while continuing to work in twelve-tone style until 1968, when his work *Credo* precipitated a scandal. *Credo*, for chorus, piano, and orchestra, juxtaposes atonal music with Bach's Prelude No. 1, in C, from the *Well-Tempered Clavier* (*Das wohltemperierte Clavier*). The music itself did not provoke authorities, for by now serialism was accepted in the Soviet Union. Not surprisingly, it was the words—the expression of Pärt's belief in Christ—which raised such ire and resulted in *Credo*'s being banned in the U.S.S.R. for ten years. *Credo* marked a watershed in Pärt's creative and spiritual life; he retreated from the world and from virtually all composing.

During his furlough Pärt returned to the roots of Western music. He studied Gregorian chant, medieval organum, and later medieval polyphony of Guillaume de Machaut. Renaissance composers—especially Johannes Ockeghem and Josquin Des Prez—served as inspirations in Pärt's quest for his own compositional voice. One hallmark of medieval and Renaissance polyphony is that it was not conceived harmonically. When chords occurred they were not planned as chords; a chord was merely the result of a simultaneous meeting of two or more melodic lines. This is significant for Pärt's later development.

In 1971 a transitional work, Symphony No. 3, punctuated Pärt's silence; also, in the early 1970s he became a Russian Orthodox. Finally, in 1976, with a piano piece—*Für Alina*—Pärt emerged from his silence with a completely new style he called "tintinnabuli."

> Tintinnabulation is like this.... I have discovered that it is enough when a single note is beautifully played. This one note, or a silent beat, or a moment of silence, comforts me. I work with very few elements—with one, with two voices. I build with the most primitive materials—with the triad, with one specific tonality. The three notes of the triad are like bells. And that is why I called it tintinnabulation.[1]

Pärt had found his voice, and "tintinnabuli" is the highly original style—employed mostly in sacred choral works—that has earned him renown.

Despite being Russian Orthodox, Pärt composed choral works for Catholic use. The year 1977 was a year rich in such works composed in "tintinnabuli" style, including *Cantate Domino*, a lively setting of Psalm 96 (95), and *Missa Sillabica*, a complete setting of the Mass, including the Dismissal,

---

1   Quoted in Paul Hillier, *Arvo Pärt* (Oxford: Clarendon Press, 1997), 87.

lasting about sixteen minutes, thus making it suitable for liturgical use.

The *Berliner Messe* was composed for the 1990 Catholic Days in Berlin, where Pärt and his family had immigrated in 1980. The Mass, for vocal quartet and organ, premiered in a liturgical context. From 1991 to 1992 Pärt revised *Berliner Messe* and rescored it for chorus and string orchestra. In 1996 the composer revised it yet again, this time going back to voices and organ, but incorporating revisions he had made to the orchestral version. In *Berliner Messe* Pärt did not set the Dismissal; instead he included three items from the Pentecost Propers—*Alleluia Emitte Spiritum, Alleluia Veni Sancte Spiritus,* and the Sequence *Veni Sancte Spiritus.*

This discussion has featured Latin-texted choral works of Arvo Pärt, but some others include *Sieben Magnificat Antiphonen* (1988), German-language settings of the "O Antiphons," sung during Advent Vespers December 17–23. Pärt has also composed English-texted works, including *I Am the True Vine* (1996), a setting of John 15:1–14, and *The Beatitudes* (1990). Personally, when I first heard Pärt's music, I thought it was monotonous, but the more I listened, the more I became captivated by its deceptive simplicity and beauty. It is a sound world that invites one to be silent and listen to the beauty that is "ever ancient, ever new."

The third Holy Minimalist is Englishman John Tavener (1944–2013). A convert to Russian Orthodoxy, Tavener composed liturgical and concert music flavored by his spiritual outlook, which though officially Eastern Orthodox, adopted over time some syncretistic elements.

Probably his best-known concert work is *The Protecting Veil,* for cello solo and string orchestra, which Tavener completed in 1988 on commission from cellist Steven Isserlis. *The Protecting Veil* refers to the Orthodox Feast of the Protecting

Veil of the Mother of God. The work consists of eight sections; in the first and eighth—both titled *The Protecting Veil*—the cello symbolizes the Virgin's eternal song, "a lyrical ikon in sound, rather than in wood," as Tavener says. Sections 2–7 follow the events of her life—Nativity, Annunciation, Incarnation, Lamentation at the Cross, Resurrection, Dormition (Assumption). This is reminiscent of Josquin Des Prez's motet *Ave Maria ... Virgo serena*, introduced above in Chapter 7.

Tavener also composed much Orthodox and Anglican sacred choral music for both concert and liturgical use. Two of his most popular choral works are *The Lamb*, a setting of Blake's poem, and *Song for Athene*, which was sung at the funeral of Diana, Princess of Wales. Readers beware, however, of his *Sollemnitas in Conceptione Immaculata Beatae Mariae Virginis* (Solemnity of the Immaculate Conception of the Blessed Virgin Mary) (2006), which is not Catholic. The composer intentionally used syncretistic texts, including Hindu, Muslim, and Native American. This is one example of Tavener's so-called "universalist" views. However, another work, *Missa Wellensis* (*Mass of Wells*) (2013), is a setting of the Latin Ordinary for the choir of Wells (Anglican) Cathedral.

The "mystic Scot" is James MacMillan (b. 1959), a composer who has successfully brought contemporary classical music to many, not by disdaining earlier trends in modern music, but by merging them with music of his own Scottish folk tradition, beautiful melodic material, and his own fervent Catholic faith. Asked about his own music in comparison with the Holy Minimalists, MacMillan responded:

> If anything, my whole compositional philosophy thrives on conflict and ambiguity.... I need that sense of drama and even theatre in my music ... music that is not mono-dimensional, music which ... has a sense of dialogue and dialectic, conflict and resolution, so that there is violence in my music whereas

with these other composers there is not, and that sometimes surprises people who think that music of a spiritual dimension should not have violence.[2]

Veni, Veni Emmanuel (1992), a concerto for percussion and orchestra featuring percussionist Evelyn Glennie, brought MacMillan early fame. Of *Veni, Veni Emmanuel* he wrote:

> On one level the work is purely abstract, in that all the musical material is drawn from the fifteenth-century French Advent plainchant. On another level it is a musical exploration of the theology behind the Advent message.[3]

The music ranges from passages for explosive percussion and brass to music of ethereal, still beauty, shot through with fleeting references to the familiar melody.

Another stunning work is MacMillan's *Seven Last Words from the Cross*, a cantata for choir and string orchestra, commissioned by BBC Television in 1993 and aired during Holy Week 1994, with each of the seven movements on a different night. Here the traditional seven last words of Christ are presented in Latin and English with music of emotional depth and beauty.

Describing himself as a "lapsed lefty,"[4] MacMillan discarded the liberation theology of his youth, which can be witnessed in works like *Búsqueda* (Search) (1988) and *Cantos sagrados* (Sacred Songs) (1989). The Jubilee Year 2000

---

2   Transcript of an interview with James MacMillan in June 1998 during the 2nd Annual Vancouver New Music Festival.
3   James MacMillan, "Notes by the Composer: Veni, Veni, Emmanuel," liner notes to "Veni, Veni, Emmanuel," Evelyn Glennie—Music of James MacMillan (Catalyst 09026-61916-2, 1993), 4.
4   Kevin McCormack, "Musica Sacra: James MacMillan and His Sacred Music for Our Time," *Catholic World Report*, November 27, 2012, https://www.catholicworldreport.com/2012/11/27/musica-sacra/.

brought a recording of some of MacMillan's liturgical music, and he also composed music for the 2010 visit of Pope Benedict XVI to England, including the Mass at Westminster Cathedral and the beatification of Cardinal Newman at Birmingham Oratory.

Most recently MacMillan has composed more concert music with religious themes, including *Miserere* (2009)—a gorgeous setting of Psalm 51 (50) commissioned by the Sixteen choir. The Pittsburgh Symphony Orchestra then commissioned MacMillan to arrange *Miserere* for orchestra, to celebrate Manfred Honeck's tenth anniversary as their music director. Titled *Larghetto for Orchestra*, it premiered in Pittsburgh on October 27–29, 2017.

Premiering in Fátima on October 13, 2017, was MacMillan's *The Sun Danced*, for soprano, chorus, and orchestra. It was commissioned for the Portuguese centennial celebration of our Lady's apparition and the miracle of the sun at Fátima. The sung texts are in Latin, English, and Portuguese, and include the words of the angel and our Lady, plus words of crowd members present at the miracle.

Last is a very recent work, MacMillan's Symphony No. 5: *Le grand inconnu*, which premiered in Edinburgh on August 17, 2019. Scored for chorus, chamber choir, and large orchestra, *Le grand inconnu* (*The Great Unknown*) denotes the mystery of the Holy Spirit. Its three movements suggest Trinitarian symbolism, but their titles refer to the Paraclete's attributes—*Ruah* (Hebrew for "wind"), *Zao* (ancient Greek for "living water"), and *Igne vel Igne* (Latin for "fire or fire"). Sacred texts in these three languages, plus English, form the basis of the choral sections. At the end of the second movement, MacMillan composed a twenty-voice motet that alludes to the forty-voice motet *Spem in alium* (Hope in other) by Thomas Tallis, James MacMillan's musical Catholic "ancestor."

Postlude

We have come to the end of our journey, or rather, pilgrimage. The musical landscape of Christendom is complex and rich, and the Catholic faith has left its mark, even indirectly, on composers and music not explicitly Catholic or even Christian.

Ancient and medieval writers had an exalted notion of music. Pythagoras, along with Plato, Aristotle, and others, forwarded the notion of music's mathematical relationship to the ordering of the cosmos, its property of instilling calm into the soul, and its effect on human behavior. Boethius and Saint Augustine transmitted to Christendom these ideas, which persisted until the Enlightenment. By the eighteenth century, writers such as Charles Burney saw music as

> [An] innocent luxury, unnecessary, indeed, to our existence, but a great improvement and gratification of the sense of hearing....
>
> As Music may be defined as the art of pleasing by the succession and combination of agreeable sounds, every hearer has a right to give way to his feelings, and be pleased or dissatisfied without knowledge, experience, or the fiat of critics.[1]

Burney's ideas clearly contradict Plato's ideas on poetic genres (see Chapter 1), as Burney promotes the right of every listener to judge music for himself. His more "earthbound" estimation of music perfectly suited a more secular age. It is in

---

1   Charles Burney, *A General History of Music* (1776–1789), 4 vols., ed. Frank Mercer (New York: Dover Publications, 1957), vol. I, 21, quoted in Piero Weiss and Richard Taruskin, *Music in the Western World: A History in Documents*, 2nd ed. (Belmont, CA: Schirmer Cengage Learning, 2008), 257.

the eighteenth century where college or conservatory music history courses start focusing more on secular instrumental music and opera, rather than church music. The Catholic approach to music—even while presenting secular genres—never neglects the spiritual orientation. For us, Bruckner's symphonies are as much an implicit expression of his Catholic faith as are his Masses and motets. Bach and Handel, although Protestants, composed music informed by Catholic heritage. Even the (Protestant) church scenes in Gershwin's opera *Porgy and Bess* and Aaron Copland's ballet *Appalachian Spring* have a remote Catholic origin.

Building on the foundation of Gregorian chant, followed by the addition of other voices resulting in harmony, the music of Western civilization is necessarily Catholic, even when its foundation is hidden. In the 1920s G. K. Chesterton affirmed: "The fact is this: that the modern world, with its modern movements, is living on its Catholic capital."[2]

It is hoped that this book has been an encouragement to learn more about the great tradition of Western classical music—the music of Christendom—and that it will encourage the reader to listen. There are many ways to listen to classical music. Naturally, live concerts are best but not always possible. Search your area for live concerts; if tickets are too expensive, investigate concerts at universities, music conservatories, and churches; these are often free or low-cost.

Currently, Catholic composers in the United States are contributing to a renascence of Catholic culture. Readers are encouraged to discover the music of Kevin Allen, Daniel Knaggs, Michael Kurek, Peter Kwasniewski, Frank La Rocca, Timothy McDonnell, and Mark Nowakowski, among others. Rather than being cultural Catholics, let us embrace the music—both old and new—of Catholic culture.

---

2   G. K. Chesterton, "Is Humanism a Religion?", in *The Thing: Why I am a Catholic* (London: Sheed and Ward, 1929), 12.

100 Essential Masterworks
of Classical Music: A Starter List

Following are one hundred masterworks that every Catholic should endeavor to know.

1. Gregorian Chant—Midnight Mass of Christmas (*Missa Dominus dixit*)
2. Gregorian Chant—*Salve Regina* (solemn tone)
3. Gregorian Chant Sequence—*Victimæ paschali laudes* (Easter)
4. Hildegard of Bingen—*Alleluia. O virga mediatrix*
5. Bernart de Ventadorn—*Can vei la lauzeta mover*
6. *Llibre vermell—O Virgo splendens*
7. Perotinus—*Viderunt omnes* (organum quadruplum)
8. Guillaume de Machaut—*Douce dame jolie*
9. Guillaume de Machaut—*Messe de Nostre Dame*
10. Anonymous—*Deo gracias Anglia* ("Agincourt Carol")
11. John Dunstable—*Quam pulchra es*
12. Guillaume Du Fay—*Nuper rosarum flores/Terribilis est locus iste*
13. Josquin Des Prez—*Ave Maria . . . virgo serena*
14. Giovanni Pierluigi da Palestrina—*Missa Æterna Christi munera*
15. Giovanni Pierluigi da Palestrina—*Super flumina Babilonis*
16. Thomas Tallis—*Salvator mundi*
17. William Byrd—*Hæc dies*

18. Tomás Luis de Victoria—*O vos omnes*
19. John Dowland—*Lachrimae, or Seven Tears* (1604)
20. Claudio Monteverdi—*L'Orfeo*
21. Claudio Monteverdi—*L'incoronazione di Poppea* (*The Coronation of Poppea*)
22. Claudio Monteverdi—*Vespers of the Blessed Virgin* (*Vespro della beata Vergine*)
23. Henry Purcell—*Dido and Aeneas*
24. Antonio Vivaldi—*The Four Seasons* (*Le quattro stagioni*)
25. Johann Sebastian Bach—Mass in B minor
26. Johann Sebastian Bach—*Saint Matthew Passion* (*Matthäus-Passion*)
27. George Frideric Handel—*Messiah*
28. George Frideric Handel—*Water Music*
29. Franz Joseph Haydn—Symphony No. 100 (Military)
30. Joseph Haydn—*Missa in Angustiis*, in D minor (*Lord Nelson Mass*)
31. Wolfgang Amadeus Mozart—Piano Concerto No. 27, in B-flat major
32. Wolfgang Amadeus Mozart—Symphony No. 41, in C major (Jupiter)
33. Wolfgang Amadeus Mozart—Requiem
34. Wolfgang Amadeus Mozart—*The Marriage of Figaro* (*Le nozze di Figaro*)
35. Wolfgang Amadeus Mozart—*Don Giovanni*
36. Ludwig van Beethoven—Symphony No. 5, in C minor, Op. 67
37. Ludwig van Beethoven—Symphony No. 6, in F major, Op. 68 (*Pastoral*)
38. Ludwig van Beethoven—Piano Concerto No. 4, in G major, Op. 58
39. Ludwig van Beethoven—Fantasia in C minor, Op. 80 (Choral Fantasy)
40. Franz Schubert—*Erlkönig* (*Erlking*)

41. Franz Schubert—*Die schöne Müllerin*
42. Hector Berlioz—*Symphonie fantastique*
43. Gioachino Rossini—*The Barber of Seville* (*Il barbiere di Siviglia*)
44. Alexander Borodin—String Quartet No. 2
45. Modest Musorgsky—*Pictures at an Exhibition*
46. Nikolai Rimsky-Korsakov—*Scheherazade*
47. Frédéric Chopin—Nocturne in D-flat, Op. 27, No. 2
48. Frédéric Chopin—Mazurka in B-flat major, Op. 7, No. 1
49. Robert Schumann—*Liederkreis,* Op. 39
50. Robert Schumann—*Carnaval,* Op. 9
51. Franz Liszt—*Années de pèlerinage* (*Years of Pilgrimage*)
52. Richard Wagner—*Der Ring des Nibelungen* (*Das Rheingold, Die Walküre, Siegfried, Götterdämmerung*)
53. Richard Wagner—*Parsifal*
54. Giuseppe Verdi—*La traviata*
55. Giuseppe Verdi—*Otello*
56. Giuseppe Verdi—Requiem
57. Anton Bruckner—Symphony No. 9
58. Anton Bruckner—*Os iusti*
59. Johannes Brahms—*Die Mainacht*
60. Johannes Brahms—3 *Intermezzi* for Piano, Op. 117
61. Johannes Brahms—Symphony No. 1, in C minor
62. Antonin Dvořák—Symphony No. 9 ("From the New World")
63. Antonin Dvořák—"American" String Quartet, in F major, Op. 96
64. Antonin Dvořák—Slavonic Dances, Op. 46
65. Pyotr Ilyich Tchaikovsky—*Romeo and Juliet* (fantasy overture)
66. Gabriel Fauré—*Le secret*
67. Gabriel Fauré—Requiem
68. Gustav Mahler—Symphony No. 2, in C minor ("Resurrection")

69. Richard Strauss—*Don Juan*
70. Claude Debussy—*Prélude à l'après-midi d'un faune* (*Prelude to the Afternoon of a Faun*)
71. Claude Debussy—3 *Nocturnes* (for orchestra)
72. Maurice Ravel—*Le tombeau de Couperin*
73. Maurice Ravel—Piano Concerto in G major
74. Sergei Rachmaninov—*Rhapsody on a Theme of Paganini*
75. Sergei Rachmaninov—Vespers (All-Night Vigil)
76. Igor Stravinsky—*The Firebird* (*L'oiseau de feu*)
77. Igor Stravinsky—*The Rite of Spring* (*Le sacre du printemps*)
78. Giacomo Puccini—*Tosca*
79. Giacomo Puccini—*La bohème*
80. Edward Elgar—"Enigma" Variations
81. Edward Elgar—*The Dream of Gerontius*
82. Ralph Vaughan Williams—*Five Variants of Dives and Lazarus*
83. Ralph Vaughan Williams—*Fantasia on a Theme of Thomas Tallis*
84. Ralph Vaughan Williams—*The Lark Ascending*
85. George Gershwin—*Rhapsody in Blue*
86. Aaron Copland—*Appalachian Spring*
87. Maurice Duruflé—Requiem
88. Francis Poulenc—*Dialogues des Carmélites*
89. Olivier Messiaen—*Le banquet céleste*
90. Olivier Messiaen—*Quartet for the End of Time* (*Quatuor pour la fin du temps*)
91. Sergei Prokofiev—*Romeo and Juliet*
92. Sergei Prokofiev—*Alexander Nevsky*
93. Dmitri Shostakovich—Symphony No. 5
94. Henryk Górecki—Symphony No. 3 (*Symphony of Sorrowful Songs*)
95. Henryk Górecki—*Totus tuus*
96. Arvo Pärt—*Sieben Magnificat Antiphonen*

97. John Tavener—*The Protecting Veil*
98. James MacMillan—*Seven Last Words from the Cross*
99. James MacMillan—*Miserere*
100. James MacMillan—Symphony No. 5: *Le grand inconnu* (*The Great Unknown*)